FEED YOUR FUTURE

Morsels on Building a Meaningful Career

Caroline Gadaleta

By Caroline Gadaleta

Inspired Forever Books
Dallas, Texas

Feed Your Future

Morsels on Building a Meaningful Career

Inspired Forever Books

Dallas, Texas

(888) 403-2727

https://inspiredforeverbooks.com

"Words with Lasting Impact"

Library of Congress Control Number: 2022906029

Paperback ISBN 13: 978-1-948903-55-4

Hardcover ISBN: 978-1-948903-64-6

Printed in the United States of America

Disclaimer: The information in this book is intended to furnish users with general information on matters that they may find to be of interest. The content shared on these pages is not intended to replace or serve as substitute for any audit, advisory, tax or other professional advice, consultation, or service.

Don't miss the new life growing on your vine.

For Frank, Shelby, and Jessie.

ACKNOWLEDGEMENTS

I would like to first acknowledge my husband, Frank, for being my number one supporter and advocate through the many life changes and challenges that became the inspiration for this book. Also, my daughters Shelby and Jessie, who inspire me each and every day to question the status quo and push for change. My mother-in-law, Jessie Gadaleta, and niece, Danielle Ceruzzi, for pitching in heavily to ensure my girls were taken care of when I went back to work. My friend and mentor Mike Algiere, who was a lifeline throughout the pandemic and talked me through many of my career quandaries in recent years. Danielle Rudolph, for always validating my observations in the workplace. My wonderful LinkedIn network, for reading my posts, liking them, and commenting on them—and most of all for their private messages encouraging me to keep writing. Eva Smith, for calling me out of the blue to say, "I think you have a book." And Michelle Morse, for making the process easy!

TABLE OF CONTENTS

ABOUT THE AUTHOR

Caroline Gadaleta is a NYC-based wife of one, mom of two, and mentor of many. She has spent her career in commercial real estate honing managerial and leadership skills across a variety of high-impact roles. In this book, she takes obvious, everyday occurrences and turns them into lessons on confidence, attitude, career, management, mentorship, and leadership to help you feed your future. You will see through her own experiential lens how you, too, can learn from your daily travels. Or simply from hers!

INTRODUCTION

Way back in 2003, when dinosaurs roamed the earth, I left a really great job I loved. I had spent more than ten years since college working and educating myself in NYC, building a successful career in commercial real estate. By 2003, I was the assistant vice president of real estate for a major publishing company, executing one hundred lease transactions per year across multiple US markets from NYC to Peoria to San Francisco. I even had an office overlooking Central Park!

My husband and I had recently welcomed our first beautiful baby girl, and my twelve-hour day (including commute) away from her was getting to me. I approached my company about possible work from home or part time, and the answer was a resounding "No"—not possible. So I packed away my suits and heels and became a suburban mom full time. It felt like my dream of building an amazing career was over. But instead of giving up, during the next eight years, I did everything from consulting to community service, taking as many leadership roles as possible while spending most of my days raising two lovely daughters. When both girls were neatly tucked away in full-time elementary school, the opportunity presented itself for me to return to full-time work! I rejoined a company I had been with early in my career, JLL. Although I took a slight step back in title and salary to make this happen, it felt like the right move. It was also an opportunity to reconnect with some of the great colleagues I had left behind who were still growing their careers there—all good stuff. While my main focus was to build back what I had lost over the past eight years, my family still came first, and I continued to volunteer for class parent and Girl Scout Cookie chair every year. In my mind, the job was very much secondary to my family responsibilities.

Something happened shortly after I made this leap back to the corporate world. At a company holiday party, I found myself surrounded by a younger generation looking at me with hope in their eyes. They started saying things like "You are my mentor" and "You've got it all, and I want to be like you." (Oh, how I had them fooled!) I suddenly realized my purpose here was not just to bring home the bacon so my family could afford more fun stuff, including vacations and college tuition. A new purpose had been revealed: inspire, mentor, and build the next generation of leaders.

Fast-forward to 2018, when I had achieved a certain amount of success as an account director at JLL. I was leaving a great role on one account to start a global role with a new client. I posted something on LinkedIn about leaving my team, and it took off. Suddenly ten thousand people had read my post. I uploaded a photo of the team, and eighteen thousand people viewed it. There was something there.

I realized at that moment the power of the written word in providing inspiration. The stories contained in this book come from all different periods of my life, and my hope is to inspire courage and confidence in leaders and managers. By sharing the lessons I have learned, I hope to encourage my readers to think differently, dig deeper, and most of all bring *all* their knowledge and experience to building their careers. It's not just about your work experience! It's about *life experience*. We can take morsels from all areas of our lives and turn them into teaching moments for ourselves, our peers, and our colleagues. Perhaps even for our children.

By the way, that company I worked for back in 2003 doesn't exist anymore. After all, dinosaurs did eventually become extinct. . .

CHAPTER ONE:
Grow Your Confidence

In my experience, confidence is *everything*. The happiest, most successful people I have come across are those who have been able to cast aside the scarecrows in their lives, hold their heads high, and plow through whatever challenges they face with agility and grace. How do they do it? Confidence is not out of reach for anyone. In fact, it's right there in your heart, waiting to emerge. For some people, it comes easily. For others, it requires construction. By the way, one thing to keep in mind: Success is how *you* define it. Not how someone else does.

Building confidence is important. It can be done one step at a time. A bunch of small wins can give you the courage to take slightly larger risks, and so forth. And courage is the number one most fundamental quality necessary for becoming a confident person!

Confidence can "crop up" in the most unexpected ways. While planting my garden last spring, I was reminded of a funny experience.

I was perusing the pansies at my local garden stand when a couple approached me with questions. After the third question, it dawned on me.

"Oh wait—do you think I work here?" I asked.

And they said, "Yes! You look like you know what you're doing."

Suddenly, another stranger's voice boomed across the begonias: "I thought you were a landscape architect!" My thumb is barely chartreuse, so to be confused with an expert in the field (pardon the pun) of gardening was a surprise to say the least. But it got me thinking about confidence as an incredibly important characteristic of successful people. It turns out my experience planting annuals in the yard for the past fifteen years had enabled me to develop an air of confidence around gardening products—enough for perfect strangers to think I might actually have some expertise.

In the context of the business world, or whatever world you work in, showing that confidence could be the key to your success. A few tricks I suggest:

- Shake off those scarecrows! Are you letting fear keep you from achieving your goals? Shake it off!

- Evict the confidence busters. Someone once said, "Don't let anyone live in your head rent-free." Turn criticism into inspiration, and prove them wrong!

- Bank your wins. It is important to be conscious of the things you need to accomplish on a daily basis, no matter how minute. Having a checklist makes you accountable. And you will be amazed at how good you feel when you draw a line through each task. It will inspire confidence—I promise!

- Be prepared. Do your homework if you are heading into a meeting with a person who might sap your confidence. You will be far more relaxed than if you try to wing it.

- Surround yourself with support. The people in your midst have the power to build *you* up. It helps if they believe in you—and if they believe in you more than you believe in yourself, even better! They cheer you on and ensure you are doing all of the above and more.

- You don't have to be an expert; you simply need to trust in your experience and ability to get things done. And apparently it also helps to walk around giving the impression you know what you are doing, even when you don't!

Build Your Confidence

» Shake Off Those Scarecrows!

Have you ever noticed how confident people seem fearless? You may wonder, *How do they do that?* No doubt they *do* have fear, but they have overcome it, at least for that moment. It's easy to get intimidated by others' success and to worry you might not measure up. When I was twenty-something and up for a big promotion to replace a colleague who had recently been named Manager of the Year at our company, I certainly had the skills and knowledge to take that next step. But I expressed trepidation (*loudly*) about filling those shoes to my then-boyfriend (now-husband!). He told me to "Be Tino Martinez." I was puzzled. He explained that Tino Martinez had been in a similar situation in the 1990s.

Don Mattingly was considered one of the all-time greatest first basemen, having spent fourteen years on the NY Yankees. He was Donnie Baseball after all! When he retired, everyone said, "How will anyone replace Donnie Baseball?" Not possible! Tino Martinez joined the team in 1996, replacing Don Mattingly at first base. He helped lead the team to World Series Championships in 1996, 1998, 1999, and 2000. Donnie Baseball had been a true champion in his own right, but he'd never won a World Series. While it can be argued that Tino never received the accolades received by Don Mattingly, he clearly showed that he was a huge talent and able to shine in different ways as part of an amazingly winning team. So next time you get intimidated by another person's reputation or fear you may not be able to live up to established expectations, take this advice: Be Tino Martinez!

Children can often provide great inspiration to adults through their innocence. We can learn much from them if we put ourselves in their shoes. "Bear" with me for a moment. When my daughter was little, she had a friend who was deathly afraid of dogs. Lock-the-dog-in-a-bedroom-when-she-comes-over type of afraid. At the time, we were all in a ballet carpool together. I happened to know that the ballet teacher, Miss Melanie, had a big, fluffy chow chow dog named Teddy Bear. So I wondered how this little friend of ours would react.

The first time I drove them to ballet, the girls ran into the studio, and I followed. When I rounded the corner in the hallway inside, I saw my daughter's dog-fearing friend petting Teddy Bear. I looked at her and said, "I thought you were afraid of dogs?"

She turned her tiny face to me, and as I gazed into her sweet yet totally serious baby-blue eyes, she said, "He's not a dog. He's a bear." Oh!

What is the purpose of fear anyway? It gets in the way of so many things. It could have prevented a joyful moment between a little girl and a fluffy dog. (I still have not reconciled that a bear could be less scary than a dog—innocence!) In this case, ignorance was bliss, and most adults don't have the ability to ignore the reality of a scary situation. What we *can* do, however, is look past what we fear to the potential (wonderful) outcome on the other side. With a little trust and faith, accepting a challenge can be a step toward building the strength we need for confidence so we can put aside our fears and get to the good stuff. The joy of life—whether it is a career move, learning something new, or joining an organization—is attainable when fear falls away!

» Evict the Confidence Busters

A high school teacher of mine unwittingly changed the course of my life. She wrote in my college recommendation that I would "never be class president" followed by a "however" and a compliment I can't remember now because I have always been focused on the class president thing. I did run for class president once—against an incumbent whose father was a popular teacher and whose older brothers had also been class president. So my loss was likely due not entirely to my failings as a candidate but rather to a mix of factors. (Also, my opponent hosted a very fun "New Coke Challenge" taste test—it was 1985—which gave him a bump at the polls. His closest friend ran the school soda machine, so he had "access.") He bested me in the race, but I beat him at our favorite Atari game, *Pitfall*, multiple times. We are all still friends to this day. But I digress . . .

The comment my teacher wrote had a huge impact. It was the inspiration I needed as I set out to prove I could lead and lead well. There is power in proving someone wrong, especially when they challenge the extent of your skills and capabilities.

People will say dumb things about you. Even if you are "totally awesome." (Sorry, the high school reference has me still stuck in the '80s.) You can get down about it, or you can rise above it and show yourself the truth. The last time I saw that teacher, I was working a crappy retail job at the mall right after college. She couldn't have been impressed. But who cares? I believed in me then as I do now—do you believe in you?

Tearing down is easier than building up, and there are dem-olition teams everywhere at the ready to crush your spirit. Each month I host a team meeting at which I share a quote of the month. In honor of Pride Month in 2021, I decided to share a Gertrude Stein quote: "You look ridiculous if you dance. You look ridicu-lous if you don't dance. So you might as well dance." What this means to me is there will be people critiquing you at every turn, no matter what you do. So get those people out of your head, and go do you! Don't let what others say or think get in the way of enjoying your life.

Unfortunately, your peers, coworkers, friends, and even family have the power to steal your confidence instead of boosting it.

During college, I worked for campus catering. I earned five dollars an hour serving faculty and distinguished guests steak and twice-baked potatoes in the university dining room. The staff was generally a mix of students, but periodically a "real person" from town would join us. One time a new face appeared—a single mom in her early forties. The small talk ensued during our shift break, and I asked about her child.

She scoffed and said, "She's some kind of honor student. Gets all As."

I said, "Oh, that is amazing! You must be very proud."

"Not really. She's going to think she is better than me. I don't like that." My heart broke at that moment for her daughter—life is hard but even harder when those around you aren't supportive.

I sometimes wonder what happened to that young straight-A student—probably in her early forties now herself. I hope she rose above her mom's insecurities. It reminds me there will always be barriers: biases, difficult relationships, insecure leaders, finances. Overcoming adversity builds strength and fosters growth. It sounds like this young girl had some barriers herself—I certainly did my best to coach her mom that night, with my twenty-one-year-old wisdom. I told her, "Your daughter's success is a reflection of you." I hope it resonated. I truly do.

I recently watched for the first time (late to the party, I know) the speech in *Rocky Balboa* from Rocky to his son. If you haven't seen it, it's a good one. The gist of it is life will continue to deliver hits to you. It will beat you to your knees sometimes. You have to be able to take the hits and keep coming back stronger. And don't let people tell you what you are worth—you know you are great, talented, and amazing.

In my mind, if you can gather those hits and convert them to rocket fuel, you can make your career (life!) take off! By the way, those people who try to knock you down? Surprise! They don't matter. In fact, if you get a chance to move away from them, you will leave them in the dust. Trust me.

Listen to Rocky. Come back harder, and win. That's what I am going to do to continue building my confidence—how about you?

» Bank Your Wins

Have you ever heard the saying "You haven't lived till you've mowed the lawn"? Of course you haven't—no one ever said that! But the other day when I was mowing the lawn, it occurred to me that it might be true. Am I saying house (and lawn) ownership is the key to happiness? *No way.* In fact, I am sure there are many out there who would argue "quite" to the contrary. No, what I mean is that getting out there and doing something that has tangible results can be truly uplifting and joyful. A sense of accomplishment can inspire confidence for the next task or project. And from there, you build a reputation, a career, a brand for yourself. Too many of us get caught up in minutiae, completing low-value, useless tasks that satisfy a client, a family member, a boss. But as soon as you are done, there are more tasks where that came from. So you need to design for yourself action plans that will provide results that make *you* feel good and help *you* grow. And don't be intimidated by this—an action plan can be as simple as a checklist. The key is to outline the things that you would like to accomplish that will add value to *your* life.

Speaking of *sense of accomplishment*, setting goals is critical when pursuing success. Setting *achievable* goals every day is one way to put yourself on the right path toward loftier ambitions. Each day, I write down three things I definitely want to accomplish before five o'clock. They can be as small as replying to an email or placing a phone call. These less significant but important achievements help me build momentum for the bigger projects I need to tackle. And that momentum helps to drive success!

About four years ago, a shingle fell off my house. I found it in my vegetable garden, looked up, and saw it had come loose from a position directly below the bedroom window. I brought it inside with the intent of reattaching it. That shingle sat on the counter, then the shelf, for a very long time. Finally, on a beautiful spring day last year, I decided it was time. Hammer in hand, I reattached the shingle. Five minutes. Ahem—four years and five minutes. Why do we do this to ourselves? I will never understand why I put this simple task off for four years. But what I will say is that I was very satisfied with the result.

Do you have small tasks you need to complete? Isn't today as good as any other day to cross them off the list?

Seeing the fruits of your labor can (and should) be energizing. In my business, many of our efforts are reactive because that is simply the nature of what we do. So it's important to give yourself the opportunity to achieve something every single day. I'm not talking about big stuff. It's little things like making a call to a contact you haven't connected with in a while. Or reviewing and rewriting your to-do list. Or reading an article to learn something new. These are all things that can be done in ten minutes or less but that will give you a sense of accomplishment. The positive energy you derive will spur you on to do something else proactive, and so on. Try it.

Okay, maybe mowing the lawn isn't all it's cracked up to be. But the day I did it (about three weeks too late), it was a grueling exercise and took way too long, but at the end we had five bags of cut grass, a beautiful lawn, and a couple of beers to celebrate the accomplishment. Not too shabby. And yes—don't forget to reward yourself for your accomplishments. It will give you something to look forward to the next time. Cheers to that!

» Be Prepared

One of my favorite and best managers (ever) taught me to "be prepared." He never actually said those words—I put them in quotes for emphasis. He merely modeled the behavior of being prepared. All the time. His desk was clear and his email inbox organized. He had time every day to take a break and chat, make us laugh, and then return to his corner office overlooking Central Park. Granted, this was before the age of smartphones and digital communications taking over our lives and invading our personal space. But he was always up to date and never procrastinated, as far as I could tell. As a young professional, this behavior was foreign to me. I was barely out of business school, where late nights at the library and last-minute studying were common occurrences. Yes, all in pursuit of "being prepared," but not well planned at all.

Being prepared has been very helpful to me as I've built my career. I have witnessed lack of preparation, and while winging it can sometimes work out just fine, it eventually catches up. More than that, being prepared can bring with it enormous benefits: kudos, client satisfaction, and recognition. Also, the avoidance of heart palpitations, high blood pressure, and certainly unnecessary stress. So maybe look at it this way—being prepared might just save your life!

» **Surround Yourself with Support**

Do you have a cheerleader? I don't mean a cute uniformed girl or boy doing flips in the air and swinging pom-poms (although it might not hurt). I mean someone who thinks your ideas are great, who lifts your spirits, who builds your confidence, and who helps you believe you can face the challenges ahead. Having someone (or more than one) in your life who can boost you up is an incredibly important part of building the confidence you need to succeed. Having them in your family is helpful, but finding them outside of the people who have no choice but to love you gives more credibility to the cheering. This is not mentoring—that is a totally different topic. Cheerleaders can be peers or acquaintances or friends or people who work for you. In a typical cheerleading situation, the cheerleader actually gets *more* excited about your abilities than you! That excitement becomes contagious and sets you on fire. It's kind of a superhuman quality!

One day I saw a guy get off my train wearing a backpack made to look like Captain America's shield. I knew my kids were going to want one. But more than that, it reminded me superheroes walk among us every day. They may not have fancy names like Black Panther or Captain Marvel, but they are saving us from ourselves as we weave our way through life.

Superheroes come in all shapes and sizes. Sometimes they are the cheerleaders who pump up your confidence on a daily basis; some are colleagues who work hard to ensure you can be successful; some are family members who provide stability and love.

Shield or no shield, they are there. It's not exactly like the movies but pretty close. In my experience, help often shows up when I don't even know I need it (or, more often, when I think I don't). So thank you to all the superheroes in my life.

As you set out to build confidence in your career, just remember that you don't have to do it alone. The week before my freshman year of college, the school had organized an "Orientation in the Wilderness." In a fit of FOMO, I signed up. I pictured campfires, s'mores, singing, and a head start on making friends. Wrong!

On day one of this adventure, I found myself descending a hill with my group. We were going caving—how bad could it be? Bad. These caves were not like those I had seen on TV in *Land of the Lost*. To get through them, we lay on our backs and shimmied along with about four inches between nose and roof. Awful. I found out that day what it meant to be claustrophobic—I'd never been so scared in my life. I must have verbalized my fear because suddenly, there was a voice and a hand. One of my group mates—a kind woman named Becky—had extended her hand and told me to hold on. I grabbed that hand and never let go until I was safely aboveground again.

When scared or unprepared or both, reach for that hand, and hold on tight. There is no reason to go it alone. Strength and courage are emboldened when we fortify ourselves with others. It can be hard to ask for help—but when it appears, it is there for a reason. Take it!

You know by now confidence doesn't just "happen." When the people at the nursery thought I was a landscape architect, it was because I had gained gardening experience over more than fifteen years that enabled me to exude confidence. Like many things of value in our lives, such as relationships and careers, confidence is built over time. Sure, some people are born with more natural gusto than others, but there is no reason you can't catch up. You just need to build it one brick at a time until you have a literal fortress of confidence around you. Patience is a virtue. Good things come to those who wait. Remember *The Tortoise and the Hare*?

Slow and steady wins the race—but you must keep the pace and stay in the game to be able to come out a winner!

CHAPTER TWO:
Ace Your Attitude

Attitude is the great influencer of outcomes. It can have an enormous effect on success. When I think about the highest performers on my team, those with the best attitudes come to mind. That is partly due to our being in the service business, where we are client facing every minute of every day. But keeping it positive while completing daily routines is critical to any individual's success. *If people want to be around you, they will want to keep you around!*

What Are the Key Components of Attitude That Breed Success?

> » **Adaptability**

I love the show *Bar Rescue*. My first introduction to it was when I was an account manager working with Diageo, the number one premium spirits company in the world. At the time, their brands were often featured prominently in the show. Jon Taffer, the larger-than-life star who creates stunning bar turnarounds, certainly has a unique style. He is a veritable bull in a china shop—the drama he creates is effective and typically instills just enough fear in the bar owners to get them to buy into the turnaround plans. The owners are often highly resistant to change and frankly need to be put on their heels.

It turns out Jon is second chance incarnate—a physical manifestation of something we all need from time to time: an opportunity to try again. I have benefitted from this kind of generosity in my life and am sure you have too. We don't always get it right the first time. In fact, we, as imperfect human creatures, quite often don't.

On one of the episodes I watched, Jon transformed a bar, but unfortunately after a few months, the owner decided to trash the new ideas and pursue his own flawed agenda. The bar has since closed. It turns out that when the bar owners have the right attitude and are willing to accept Jon's critiques and suggestions, they achieve success. He is an expert with experience—it makes sense. To those getting the second chance—well-meaning people are ready to help. Be open to and accepting of changes that could bring you true success!

Sometimes change is tough to picture. I remember having a brief chat with myself back in middle school, in which I said, "There is *no way* Jordache Jeans will ever go out of style." Even at that young age, I knew it was unlikely, but I couldn't picture such a popular brand ever losing favor. And yet—do you see any Jordache still around? I think I saw some at a thrift store recently. Or perhaps on eBay.

Change is inevitable and often unpredictable. As an example, it is truly amazing to me how static workplace design was for literally generations, and now companies spend zillions of dollars trying to figure out the trends before it's too late and more change has taken hold. Who would have ever thought senior management would sit in open-plan environments? In my twenties, I had an office overlooking NYC's Central Park. Twenty years later, I didn't even have an assigned seat!

Sometimes the refusal to change breeds missed opportunities. I was at the bank the other day and noticed they still have those pens tethered to the desk—the same ones they have had for my entire life. I know of other banks that have pens bearing their logo that are not tied down. I suppose the idea is that if you take the pen, it turns into a marketing tool every time you or someone you are with sees it. Simple yet brilliant. To the banks with the tether, I want to say, set those pens free! Let me steal your pen! By the way, those tethered pens still get stolen all the time *and* are expensive to replace. You could probably purchase dozens of branded "free" pens for the price of one that is tied down. Interestingly, when I was at the ATM that day, I picked up the poor helpless pen and turned it over, and do you know what was printed on it? "Staples"! A missed opportunity indeed. Suddenly, I was thinking about what I needed at Staples.

Adaptability is a major key to building a positive attitude. If you can keep up with the changes, you will be okay. It is important to constantly sharpen your skills, focusing on your areas of strength and value add. Continuous learning on the job or in a classroom or some hybrid of both can help. But if you can't or don't want to adapt, you may fade away—just like that cool old pair of Jordache Jeans!

» **Resilience**

You had a bad day. So what? Shake it off. Move on. Okay, maybe have a little pity party for a maximum of twenty-four hours. (I find it helps.) But then, rise above, and go back to a positive way of thinking. My husband made me chuckle the other night when I came home and announced I'd had a bad day. In his best Dana Carvey/George H. W. Bush impression, he told me to "stay the course." I thought about Bush's "thousand points of light" phrase and realized yes, there is much more good than bad out there for me today.

The next day I went to my husband and said, "I am feeling positive."

He said, "I am too."

And later that day, I received two bits of news that made me feel *extremely* positive. Keep in mind I also got plenty of challenges in my inbox that day. But I focused on the positives, and it made all the difference.

Being proactive extends to everything in life, including managing your attitude and outlook. Bringing negativity to the table is not cool. Bringing solutions for overcoming challenges you are facing—that is cool. So if you have a bad day, it's okay. But find a way (quickly!) to ensure the next day is better.

I recently was having a bad day, but of course I soldiered on. And on one of my calls, I was talking to a revered colleague about golf because we had seen each other recently at a golf outing. I told her the thing I hated most about golf was the pressure—those people behind you who were annoyed that they had to wait because somehow things had started to back up. What she said next resonated. Greatly.

She said, "No one plays well every day. Even people who are great have bad days out on the golf course. And it's okay. So sometimes when you drive the ball poorly, you just have to pick it up and move it to where another better ball is and start over."

Huh. Well, this makes sense. There are good days and bad days, but one bad day doesn't mean you are worthless or terrible at what you are doing. It just means you might need to try again. Or find a different starting point and reboot!

One morning on the train as I battled an eyelash that was insisting on stabbing me in the eyeball over and over again, I thought about how irritating microscopic problems can be, especially when they don't get resolved. We have all faced difficult issues that started out tiny and then mushroomed into behemoths that suddenly took over our lives. Hopefully it doesn't happen often, but even if you try not to "sweat the small stuff," sometimes addressing those issues head-on can save countless headaches down the road. I have a few bubbling beneath the surface right now, and I need to knock them out *ASAP* to avoid pain later on.

I won the battle on the train, by the way. I was tempted to give up at first because the lighting was bad, I didn't have a proper mirror, and my makeup was getting messy. But I stuck with it, and the tiny dagger disappeared. Another challenge faced and resolved. Now, on to the real ones, eyes wide open . . .

» Humility and Modesty

I attended a presentation by a motivational speaker, and one of his morsels was "Be humble but not modest." To me, humility and modesty are two great virtues that go together. I think his message was "Don't let your good work go unnoticed." Fair enough.

One of my favorite family movies to watch over and over again is *Jack and Jill*, an Adam Sandler original in which he plays male and female twins. Truly hilarious. One big surprise is that Al Pacino, one of the greatest and most serious film actors of all time (my opinion), plays a major role as himself. But his "character" is a caricature of his real self, falling in love with the annoying twin sister (impossible!) and agreeing to rap and dance in a Dunkin' Donuts commercial. Did you ever think the star of *The Godfather*, *Scarface*, and *Carlito's Way* could perform comedy in a format where he was the human punch line? In *Jack and Jill*, Al Pacino teaches us a lesson in humility by playing this nonsensical role. He pokes enormous fun at himself—something most would never expect from him—and pulls it off, handily. The fact that it is Al Pacino makes it even funnier because he is such an intensely serious actor.

Humility is something I look for in my leaders and employees. Ego can be a huge barrier to showing humility and can be an indicator of fragility the individual is trying to hide. People like to see the humanity in others, and by showing some vulnerability, we can open doors to better connections. This will surely be a focus of mine in the future!

I was thinking about two other highly accomplished yet humble and definitely modest people I have come across in my travels. One was an older gent who volunteered with me on Mondays counting the church offering and sharing great conversation. He also spent many days driving the sick, the lonely, and the elderly around town for various appointments and such. I later found out he was the former president of the March of Dimes and had invented the walk-a-thon. He never told me that.

The second person was quietly the CFO of a major financial institution in NYC and also the mom of one of my daughter's friends. Most of the parents had no clue about her alter ego, but her husband let it slip one day. When I was organizing volunteers for the school fair, she asked how she could help. I'm no dummy—I put her in charge of the outdoor-barbecue cash box, and she repeated that role for five years. Best cashier ever!

Keep that humility and modesty coming—but don't let your good work go unnoticed! It's okay to speak up if you win an award and no one made recognition of it, for example. It's not just you who needs to see it—chances are, others are watching you and your success and will be inspired by your win. With regard to humility, I used to tell my staff who were managing facilities for a large corporate client, "Act like an owner, but don't act like you own the place." You can easily carry yourself with assurance and confidence without arrogance.

» Compromise

"Meet Me Halfway"—a song by Kenny Loggins from the '80s with a message. Meeting halfway is good for all kinds of relationships: with friends, family, and even clients. But sometimes you have to take it a step further and meet them where they are.

I learned this on vacation with my teenage daughters. Regarding social media, I've been on Facebook (for old folks) and LinkedIn (huh?) for years, but then I relented and joined them on Instagram. Their interest has since faded, even regarding their "Finsta" accounts. At a loss for ways to connect in recent months, I noted they were avid users of Snapchat. And so, I am learning to Snapchat. I met them on their platform, and it is paying off.

Negotiations don't have to be a zero-sum game. Or maybe the wins and losses won't be measured in the same way. Even though it seems like I gave in by meeting my daughters in their world,

I am reaping the rewards of connection and interaction I have needed for a while. And I'm sure they are getting some laughs at my expense, which is like gold for them. It's okay. All good.

A client recently pulled me past the halfway mark, and I survived. It really helped build the partnership, too, and produced a great result. Meet me halfway. Or not. But meet me!

» Letting Winners Win

As an undergraduate, I conducted campus tours for the Admissions Office. When we passed through the athletic facilities, I would always note that Wesleyan, my small liberal arts university in central Connecticut, was the only school to be undefeated against Michigan in football. The teams had met once in 1883, and Wesleyan had won 14–6. Fair and square. What an achievement! Now you might say, "Yeah, but . . ." Yes, I know what you are thinking. But a win is a win! And the record stands.

When my team wins a tiny piece of business, it's not going to move the needle or garner us any awards. But we give kudos all around because someone on the team drove that business home, and now it is ours, and we are proud. A win is a win. On to the next one!

From time to time, I see memes and such on social media lamenting the "everybody wins" mentality we have instilled in the younger generations. You get a medal for participating, versus the previous generations who had to "earn" their wins. No more blood, sweat, and tears! Or maybe we are looking at this all wrong. I will tell you why I think we are.

When I look around my multigenerational work environment, I see a younger generation that is focused on inclusion, wanting more people to have seats at the decision-making table—and wanting a more diverse group at that. They are aghast at some of the status quo norms we take for granted—and they push back with might. That's right; I think it could just be that . . . they want everyone to win! They don't believe the same people should always come out on top—they believe we should all have the right and, more importantly, the chance to bring home the prize.

Could it be that our efforts to make success more in reach for all children has created a generation of professionals who are okay with spreading out the wins? Could it be that simple? I'm sure there's something there. And if not, well, I am certainly content to see where this is going. I'll gladly drink that Kool-Aid—and toast their success!

Recognition is not a zero-sum game. If we are on the same team and you win, it doesn't mean I lose. It means our team produces winners, and that's good for everyone.

» Appetite for Risk

Will you be a *survivor* or a *warrior* this year? One year from now, will you say "I survived" or "Veni, vidi, vici"? It's an easy choice, really. It is a matter of perspective as well. Each new year, we all face exciting (perhaps exhausting) challenges. I would suggest hitting them head-on instead of in defensive mode. Either way, you will have to suit up in your battle gear. If you are in a leadership position, you will be setting an example for your team. They will want to follow you onto the battlefield.

Until recently when I looked back on my life, I described myself as a *survivor*. Then it suddenly dawned on me in a moment of clarity that I hadn't just "survived" all the challenges I had faced—I'd sought them out! I'd headed into the danger zone when others had said, "*Don't go!*" So many of the choices I had made from early on had not been on the straight and narrow. I had actively sought the more difficult path and gained strength along the way.

A few years ago, I put my future in the hands of my local leadership team and basically said, "Put me where you need me." I work in an outsourced service business, so we typically move around from account to account every few years. There was a new client relationship in need of a global account director, and I answered the call. It was a tough contract—unlike anything we had done before—and our company had agreed to some cost-savings commitments that were virtually unachievable and frankly outlandish. In fact, there had already been two leaders on the account. One had politely declined to move forward with it and stayed with his current role. The other had accepted the role and a few months later had proceeded to *quit*! Left the firm completely! But I had just won the Account Manager of the Year award and was feeling like my luck couldn't run out, so I said "Sure." It was a tough assignment—the first year of an outsourced contract always has its challenges, but in this case we had agreed to a model that was way outside of our comfort zone, and it pained everyone on all sides. Despite these challenges, we achieved great success and established a platform from which the team would eventually meet the contract requirements—something no one had truly expected. But it was *hard*. And painful. During that time, I often said to my colleagues, "I don't need sympathy, just understanding." I kept my attitude positive and was eventually promoted into a different business line, where my career took off in another direction. I would never have had my current opportunity if I had not jumped into the fire a few years earlier. Taking that risk paid off in spades.

While driving one morning, I saw a parent on a bicycle without a helmet. The person was trailing a small dog on a leash and was followed by an elementary school–aged child on a bike of her own. As I drove down a busy road, they emerged from a side street onto the double yellow. I thought, "Risky."

As a big believer in taking calculated risks, I wondered if this parent had thought ahead. Maybe they had and thought it seemed like a good idea on a sunny, warm day in the middle of a pandemic when families have been cooped up in their homes for hours on end. No need for me to judge. But as someone who has spent most of my career managing real estate, risk management is kind of in my DNA at this point.

Life moves forward at a snail's pace if we don't step out of our comfort zone and take risks. But taking calculated risks is the best approach, and even a *big* risk can be measured and mitigated to limit potential harm.

At a restaurant in Delaware, my father-in-law asked about something on the menu. "What is scrapple?"

The waitress said she would ask and stepped into the kitchen. She returned with this: "The chef doesn't know what's in it either."

"Okay, I'll have it!"

Now *that* was a risk. It's good to know a little bit before you dive in. By the way, he liked the scrapple. But never had it again!

Some risks are simply worth taking. I came across a sign in my travels last summer that said "Keep Off the Rocks" (not traveling, actually—just pretending to be on vacation at our local beach). It's funny to me how much we know about the risks of walking around rock outcroppings and formations, and yet we need these reminders to tell us not to do it. It's almost like humans are drawn to danger, and thankfully so, because think of how many adventures and discoveries never would have happened if we kept off the rocks every time.

These rocks in particular were pretty cool. Most likely formed during the Ice Age, they had many ridges and valleys, where little hermit crabs and snails made their homes and were discovered by small children each summer. But they got discovered only by the kids who either couldn't read or purposely defied the "Keep Off the Rocks" instruction.

In the end, I guess we have a choice. After all, it's not "illegal" to walk on the rocks. It's just not recommended. But if you don't, you will miss out. You could get hurt, but you also could be just fine. So will you keep off the rocks going forward?

Be a little daring this year. Be a warrior. Get out there, and face new challenges, bringing home some wins—big or small. Your family, friends, and colleagues—while they don't "need" to be impressed, they will be. And you will be stronger one year from now than you are today. Let's do this!

» Can-Do

Somehow, a few years ago, I found myself in charge of the dunk tank at our school's annual carnival. My charge was to secure a "high-profile" local person to be the dunkee. So, of course, I turned to a local politician who was up for reelection. I called him out of the blue one day, and do you know what his answer was? "Where and when?"

The day of the carnival arrived, and it was *freezing*. He showed up *in a suit* and said, "Where is the dunk machine?" I pointed, and he took his position. I know, I know. He was a politician, so of course he would do anything to get reelected. Maybe. But I was thoroughly impressed with his gumption—and, by the way, he helped raise thousands of dollars for our school that day because the dunk tank is one of the most popular stations no matter who is getting dunked. (And I think there may have been a parent or two from the opposing party who found it quite entertaining.)

Sometimes people are willing to do crazy things to help. They "jump right in," and isn't that great? I love when people ask me, "What do you need?" and deliver, no questions asked. I, for one, was impressed with this politician. And by the way, he is now in a much bigger government role. Good for him—and good for us!

One April while in Florida for our daughters' varsity softball spring training, as we wove in and out of ESPN and Disney Parks, I wondered, "How can I add value?" (other than the obvious—by being an ATM to my two daughters and providing basic chaperoning functions). As someone who is used to leading, I was enjoying my support role but not feeling entirely useful. Along for the ride, you might say.

And then, the morning of our planned departure, the universe delivered. We awoke to find out that our flight had been *canceled*. Not delayed, not postponed. *Poof!* The coach immediately embarked on a series of calls, which finally led to a connection with a helpful airline employee who focused on our case for a good three hours. Nothing available until the next day. I stepped in to handle the organizing of names and time slots and finalization of the delayed flight plan (twenty-nine people assigned to six different flights). Next, we needed to ensure we had rooms for the night—our existing rooms were already booked to a different group, so we had to find ten rooms near each other but ensure the chaperones lined the perimeter. Task completed, no problem. All in all, the logistics took six hours to finalize.

I was absolutely thrilled to put my organizational skills to work that day to help the team revise their plans. Sometimes the purpose takes time to reveal itself!

How Can You Work Toward a Success-Oriented Attitude?

» Manage Your Stress

Stress hates healthy living. A few years ago, during a very stressful time in my life, I went out and bought (read: ordered online) a stand-up punching bag and boxing gloves. That's right; I took up boxing. Why not? It is a great workout *and* stress reliever.

Which brings up the real topic: Are you managing your stress properly? When I was in that new global account director role, I quickly realized my stress levels were off the charts. Even though I often think of red wine as one of my best pals, I knew alcohol was not the answer to my stress-release needs. So I started running. I don't run a lot (in fact, painfully little), but I go out and do a run/walk at least three times per week. It helps a *lot*, and in fact, many of my best ideas are hatched during those sessions. I should also acknowledge that writing is a source of stress relief for me as well. The feedback I get from my readers brings sunshine to my day.

Exercise, writing, art, volunteering, cooking, creating, competing—all very wise and natural ways to combat the beast we know of as stress. Adding them to your routine can bring great satisfaction while helping you be more successful at your job. Be sure to proactively manage your stress—and don't let life give you the ole one-two punch!

» **Show Respect**

Sometimes people who feel small need to belittle others to feel big. One weekend, there was a newspaper article featuring a semi-famous person whom I once had the displeasure of knowing. I had managed an upscale building in NYC, and she had been one of our tenants. The article displayed a rags-to-riches story of a tenacious unstoppable person who had built a formidable reputation in her industry. That part was true and impressive. But all I can remember about her was that she treated my employees very badly. Worse than I have ever seen anyone treated in a professional situation. She screamed at them. She screamed at me. For no reason. Actually, there were reasons. She was breaking the rules in the building and causing safety hazards—and she didn't like being called out on it.

Treating people with dignity is a nonnegotiable for me. I don't care who you are or how famous you are. I'm glad those interactions happened at the beginning of my career to teach me that valuable lesson. Sometimes we need to see what is wrong in order to understand what is right. I have always known right from wrong, but the experience with this tenant etched in my brain and heart the passion with which I fiercely protect and support my team. So I guess perhaps I should thank her! Her reputation preceded her—to this day anyone who has worked with her will cringe at the mention of her name. Her fame was actually notoriety. She was lucky to have a knack for her business. Most of us are just normal people trying to make a living. Respect for others helps build a positive reputation and makes people want to work with you, support you, help you. Remember when I said, "If people want to be around you, they will want to keep you around"? A big part of building your career is creating a network of support around you, and treating people with respect is a surefire way to attract connections.

» Be Authentic

Who is your favorite shark on *Shark Tank*? Mine is Kevin, a.k.a. Mr. Wonderful. Every time he speaks, it makes me smile or laugh. I love all the sharks, but Kevin (to me) is the epitome of authenticity. He is the conscience standing on your shoulder, giving you the reality check you need. He is also angry, cranky, cantankerous— and the spitting image of one of my favorite bosses ever.

Kevin reminds me to be authentic—to be my true self and to not be afraid to say no or call people out or demand better. In my work, I see many areas for improvement. In fact, my greatest inspirations are my daughters—I want to leave the business world better than I found it, for them. In my roles, I have called out weak leaders who discriminate and don't understand inclusion. I have pushed for change to ensure things are more equitable and diverse in recruiting, promotions, and even presentations. It hasn't always worked out well for me—you wouldn't believe how defensive some leaders get when you call them out. (Yeah, just kidding. You would believe it.) Some have even tried to bury me. They couldn't. But you don't have to do what I have done, because you have to be you. And maybe it's just about being honest. I have seen many people brush incidents under the carpet because they don't want to make waves. I get it. We all have responsibilities to balance, and sometimes it's not worth your livelihood to make sure things are always as right as they should be. You have to weigh the risks.

Not everyone is as confident as Mr. Wonderful, but we can try. He tells us it's okay to be unfiltered and to speak our minds. Too often we tiptoe around because we don't want to offend anyone— hopefully not at the expense of achieving results. I will definitely always ensure that my employees have the freedom to be authentic in my midst. But that goes along with it too: be real, be kind, and be successful!

» Appreciate Every Day

In my teens, I walked to and from school every day, and along my path there was a jolly crossing guard at one of the intersections. Periodically on my way home, I would arrive while the stoplight was not in my favor, and we would chat, mostly about the weather.

On one of these occasions, toward the end of my senior year, I must have made a comment that I was *so done* with this small town (which I still live in, by the way) and couldn't wait to put high school behind me. He looked at me with a twinkle in his eye and a big smile on his face, saying, "But these are the best days of your life." That is *not* something any teenager wants to hear, and in fact it affected me so much that I think of it every time I pass that corner. It has haunted me for over thirty years. And looking back, I can't actually imagine anyone, except perhaps a popular girl or star athlete here or there, who would look back at the teen years that way.

And then it dawned on me recently. That twinkle in his eye was very telling. His message, whether he meant it or not, has echoed in my brain: these are the best days of my life. Every time I hear it repeat, it reminds me that life gets better and better. Every day has the opportunity to be the start of a new adventure—and perhaps the best day of your life. That sneaky man! He put that refrain in my head to remind me of the gift of life. Well played, Mr. Crossing Guard!

Speaking of school, the first day of school is always so filled with promise and excitement. Do you sometimes wish every day could be so hopeful? Wait a minute—why can't it? Even if you have something ugly cooking for the day, there is always room for positivity. I heard a motivational speaker say, "Every day is day one."

We are given this amazing opportunity to start over every day—let's use it. Any day can be your first day going forward. Go get 'em!

» Turn Challenge into Opportunity

My mom claims she dated Amy Klobuchar's dad when they were students at the University of Minnesota in the 1940s and '50s. I'm glad she didn't end up with him, much as she may now bemoan the fact that she is not the mom of a presidential candidate but possibly could have been—yes, she did say that—but I digress. I'm glad because, of course, if my mom had stayed in Minnesota, she would never have met my dad, and, well, you know the rest.

Amy Klobuchar has been very open about deep personal struggles within her family. I can imagine it must have been tough during those years. Yet look what those tough times produced: a daughter who went for the highest office in the land. Not bad. It rcminded me that difficult circumstances often help us grow and learn in ways we may not have chosen or imagined and shape us into stronger, more resilient people. Think about it—how much fruit did the easy times bear for you? Hopefully plenty, but I will bet the tough times did as well and in more meaningful ways.

It's something to consider if you find yourself in the abyss: you will rise and overcome, and you will be better prepared the next time, even if you decide a presidential run is not in your future!

» Seek Environments That Better You

One day at lunchtime, it was beautiful outside in NYC. I decided to eat my salad in the outdoor plaza by my client's building. It was enjoyable—a little people watching, a little catch-up texting with friends, and then . . . two young women sat down next to me and lit up cigarettes. I considered moving, but since I was almost done, I toughed it out as billows of smoke surrounded me.

When I reentered the building, I realized that I smelled of smoke—my hair, my clothes . . . I would have to live with this for the rest of the day. I should have moved as soon as they'd lit up. Lesson learned.

We sometimes underestimate how much our surroundings influence and stick with us. We tolerate, we tough it out, but at the end of the day, what are we gaining? Perhaps we are building strength, but if the negative side of our environment lingers with us, that negativity can potentially spread to other people. Certainly something to think about!

New York City is a town filled with wonder and surprise. One morning on my way to a meeting, I noticed a peacock feather stuck to a manhole cover as I headed up Madison Avenue. You are probably thinking it must have come from a garment, and you might be right. Or it could have made its way from Uptown.

The feather made me think of my days as a Columbia student in Morningside Heights. I lived half a block from the Cathedral of St. John the Divine at 112th Street, and every morning I would walk my dog Lucy to the church so she could see . . . the peacocks. Yes, there were multiple peacocks living on the grounds, and when you didn't see them, you could certainly hear them. Loud ugly squawks that didn't match the regal beauty of the birds.

That delicate feather reminded me that even in the harshest of environments, whether your city or your job or simply your situation, there is something that can help you find peace. I haven't seen the peacocks in years, but thinking of them puts a big smile on my face—and a spring in my step!

One environment we spend a lot of time in is our place of work. Do you want to know the number one most important factor in choosing a job? Working with good people. And I don't just mean nice people, because not everyone is *nice*, but they can still be good, honest people who care about you. That last bit is really important: people who care about *you*. If you think you can tough it out with a toxic client or boss because it will make you stronger—well, maybe it will. Or maybe it will cause trauma that will be hard to shake later on. On the flip side, working with people who are motivated to support your personal accomplishments will produce dividends beyond monetary compensation: mental health, lower stress, and, as a result, greater overall well-being. And that translates to more success, and so on. Life is short; surround yourself with the best!

Ride the Wave of Destiny

I absolutely love a good underdog story. Scrappy people never taking no for an answer, fighting their way toward their goals. *Rocky* may be one of the greatest such stories of all time. To think that a young, out-of-shape kid from the streets of Philly could become the heavyweight champion—pure fiction. Yet we are surrounded by these stories every day in real life. I used to watch *Undercover Boss* regularly and was astounded by the number of CEOs who had been raised in circumstances we tend to deem "less than ideal." It was part of the genius behind the show, because the overall purpose was to uncover the diamonds in the rough among their ranks. In my first real job, I was responsible for the hiring (and firing, unfortunately) of legal assistants in a big NYC law firm. I noted instantly that my best employees were those who had the hunger—the desire—and the attitude to succeed. It's that underdog mindset: I will face it, rise above it, and conquer it. Sometimes it may feel like a boxing match, or like a ride on a bulldozer, plowing through the barriers and blockers. But when you surround yourself with the best people and they support you every day, it feels more like riding a wave of destiny—a thrill, a challenge, and truly an adventure.

About twelve years ago, I attended a talk at our local library given by a fellow mom who had recently made great strides building a career as a photographer. My interest stemmed from wanting to restart my own career and a fascination with those types of "reboot" success stories.

The talk went as you might imagine—a brief history of life before children, the hiatus, and then a sudden launch into a new passion. Someone asked, "How did you find photography?"

Her answer struck a chord that still echoes within my soul. "I didn't find photography. Photography found me." She said it almost in disbelief—as if she was still stunned at discovering this passion within herself.

At that moment I thought, "Will my destiny find me?"

When it was time to relaunch my career, passion was less on my mind than landing a job. *Any* job, really, to get my foot (a toe, perhaps?) back in the door where my focus had lain before. But through the years since then, I have continued to wonder if I would have the same good fortune as my photographer friend.

It turns out my destiny has revealed itself as well. The path before me will require courage and strength, perseverance and dedication. I am ready! Do you think your passion will find you? Or are you lucky enough to already be in hot pursuit of your dream?

CHAPTER THREE:
Nourish Your Career

What is the difference between a job and a career? In my mind, a job is a means to an end—a stop on the "career highway"—and a career is a series of jobs with fulfillment. It checks boxes in our lives other than simply putting food on the table. It enables us to make a difference, connect with great people, build our skills, and dream of big things. Nothing says a job can't do the same, but a career ties jobs together along a trajectory. Having a career is aspirational.

Before my career interest in real estate emerged, I interviewed at one of the top management firms in NYC. I was a fresh-faced college graduate with no experience other than as a camp counselor and waitress. They had an opening for a receptionist, and I felt I had the qualifications. (I didn't.) The job was located at the Lipstick Building in NYC—I thought I had "arrived." It was my first interview ever. But I turned the job down because they were offering only one week of vacation. It was something I couldn't fathom, especially since I was alone in New York, and my family was many miles away.

I always wondered: Would I have built a career there? A few years later, it was the type of firm my classmates in business school were clamoring to get into. It seemed back then maybe I had been too shortsighted. Maybe. I was recounting this story to a colleague as we walked by the Lipstick Building the other day. The gentleman walking in front of us was clearly amused. When we came to the crosswalk, he turned and said, "They used to be my client. Very difficult company to work with!"

So thank you to the stranger on an NYC street for solving my curiosity—perhaps I did not miss out after all!

How Can You Turn a Job Into a Career?

» Own Your Future

I gleefully attended *The Cher Show* in 2019, celebrating my best friend's "milestone" birthday. So great to learn the story behind a tremendous icon of our time. Born shy, she realized her vision at an early age and set out to conquer the world. Hard work and connecting with the right people got her to where she wanted to be. But so many pitfalls along the way: Sonny owned her brand (95 percent—and his lawyer owned the other 5 percent!), she never had enough time for her children, and even with huge fame and influence, there were many naysayers out and about and around her.

Some of these themes may be familiar to you. We often give over control of our careers to others, even if unwittingly. We try to balance the demands of work, family, and downtime, and no matter how high we climb, there are people who try to push us back down. These are not issues specific to any gender, industry, or culture. They are facts of life and are obstacles to be overcome!

Cher took control of her career, fired the people who tried to keep her in a box, fought for time with her family, and answered the naysayers by winning awards in multiple disciplines. She showed she was tough, versatile, and talented. You can do it too—you don't need Bob Mackie costumes or a size 0 physique to be your best. You just need to "Believe" and go get it!

» Be Proactive

"You can't start a fire without a spark." (Thank you, Bruce Springsteen.) One small idea sets off a chain reaction. While dining with a friend and colleague, I was reminded of the time shortly after I first met her when . . . she quit! She was leaving, and we were faced with replacing her role. In a moment of clarity, I thought, "Hmm."

I went to the boss and said, "If you give me her portfolio and let me hire one assistant, I will manage all of it." That one suggestion set in motion the growth in my career that continues today. One small idea, and many happy events to follow. Listen to the inner voice telling you to make that suggestion. I got lucky, and it landed well with the first set of ears it found. If you aren't so lucky, try again. And again, if you have to! But don't give up—keep pushing forward (and let me know how you do!).

I sat behind a guy on the train once who was saving a seat for someone. Countless people stopped and asked if the seat was free, and each time he had to tell them he was saving it. I looked at the time, and the minutes to departure kept counting down. Would his friend arrive in time? He nervously looked around repeatedly and finally tried calling. Aha—so there really was a person coming. But alas, they never showed. The end of the story was that who-ever came by next, he would have to let them sit there.

I started thinking about "saving a seat"—letting opportunity pass you by. I think we all do this to a certain extent. It reminds me of a funny line from National Lampoon's *Christmas Vacation*. When the derelict cousins show up in their motor home and cry poverty, Ellen Griswold asks Cousin Catherine why Cousin Eddie has been out of work for so long. "He's holding out for a manage-ment position" is the reply.

It's an extreme example, but have you ever thought, "Why am I saving a seat?" If you wait too long and don't take a proactive approach, you may have to settle for what comes along. And it may not be what you hoped for. So define what you want, and go get it. Now!

You have seen the articles stating that people leave bad bosses, not bad jobs. A great boss can make any job seem dreamy—and the converse is true as well. I once had someone tell me if they hadn't put up with some bad bosses along the way, they would never have made it to where they are today. And that's a fair point because the reality is there could be lots of crap bosses out there, and it would take some kind of miracle to live a life without terrible bosses com-ing along once in a while.

But what of those great bosses we dream about? As much as we love them, we need to have the courage to move on from them or risk career stagnation. It's tempting to hang on—they treat you well, compensate you, give you the recognition you deserve. But they can also hold you back without realizing it, and then when they leave, what happens to you? You may have passed up opportunities that would have propelled you forward. So I would say beware of the bad boss and the great boss. In either situation, what is most important is your growth and development as an individual. When that starts to be compromised, start looking around. The future *you* is waiting!

» Seek Help

Always have someone review your résumé before sending it out. When I was in college, I had a campus job as a student manager at one of the food services. Every night, one of us had to be "on call" in the event a worker did not show up. So naturally, I wrote on my résumé that I "provided on-call services." Ugh. A good friend rooted that one out for me, thank goodness (but not before it had been distributed minimally). So take that extra step, and get that extra set of eyes on your résumé . . . before you start giving the (sometimes very) wrong impression!

» Learn From Others

Something really fun about watching old movies is seeing stars before they became "someone" just trying to prove themselves and hone their craft. I watched a movie in which Ryan O'Neal was the star, but Tommy Lee Jones was a side character—he became an Oscar winner and multi-award winner and nominee over the course of his career. I remember watching Meg Ryan as Betsy on

As the World Turns, and then suddenly, she was the "it" girl of '80s and '90s romantic comedies—also a big-time award winner and nominee.

Three summers ago, my daughter started her first camp counselor job. I, too, was a camp counselor in my teens and twenties, at the same camp. Those summers were part one of my education as a leader. There were schedules, behaviors, activities, emotions, challenges, and opportunities to manage every day. Negotiations were a big part of my daily routine. (I worked with middle school girls—'nough said.) There were limited resources with which to fashion the summer of a lifetime—but we did, handily. We had food, tents, marginal bathroom facilities, a beautiful lake complete with a cliff for diving, campfires, s'mores, lots of singing, and incredible friendships.

This particular camp drew campers from a wide variety of backgrounds/socioeconomic circumstances. I believe this is where the concepts of diversity and inclusion first crept into my DNA. In those years, my peers would head off to office jobs each summer to get "real-life experience." I somehow knew that summers at camp would be more impactful for me. Oh, and I was outside enjoying nature all summer!

Recently, I found out that in 1990, Lin-Manuel Miranda (creator of *In the Heights* and *Hamilton*) was one of our campers. I didn't know this for a long time, and I don't remember him. The point is that at any time, in any place, you could be in the company of genius—but you might not know it. That's a fact, and it is exciting! Keep that in mind throughout your daily travels. (BTW, I wonder if I had an influence on him?)

Oh, how I wish we could rewind the tape on some of the stars we see in the business world today—to see how they started and the growing pains but obvious potential they exhibited. Even today, as I interact with the future leaders of tomorrow, I am excited thinking about what they will do, where they will go. The good news today is we have social media and much greater documentation of "real" people than we ever had before. Keep your eye out for those shooting stars—someday you may be thinking, "Remember when. . ."

» **Appreciate Your Gifts**

I received two awards when I was a child that should have made me happier than they did. For me, despite solid efforts, there were no trophies for sports or any real "achievement" awards. Rather, the recognition I received was as follows: In 1980, I won the Attendance Award for my summer swim team. Big whoop—it was pretty embarrassing going up to get that award, I must say, when others were being glorified for their speed and countless victories. I was the dope who never missed a practice and *still* could not win a race!

The following year in 1981, I was honored with the Sportsmanship Award at my day camp. Okay, a little better, but still not Most Athletic or Best All Around Camper. I truly felt like a loser for many years because I thought these awards showed I really wasn't good at anything after all. Poor me.

And then it dawned on me, more recently than I would like to admit, these were amazing and very telling awards. Showing up and being a team player are pretty awesome qualities I am proud of. They don't necessarily garner the highest honors, but wow, I am happy someone noticed. The full picture of a person is more than skill—speed and agility will get you places, but combined with character and commitment, they will truly move you forward!

» Value Each Experience

We build skills through our experience. To me, there are two types of experience: *good experience* and *experience*. *Bad experience* doesn't exist because there is always something to be learned, and that, in and of itself, is positive.

I bussed tables at a restaurant on Fire Island in New York the summer after my freshman year of college. Four of us had the good fortune to take over my friend's parents' beach house and get jobs to keep ourselves busy during a six-week jaunt. I worked in one of the more popular restaurants, and it was an "experience." We were paid $2.50 an hour to come to the restaurant every morning to clean the vinyl tablecloths with bleach, which took about one hour. So $2.50 earned—yay! Then we arrived at four o'clock in the afternoon and worked straight through until eleven or midnight. At the end of the shift, my feet felt like I had walked a mile on hot coals. There was a serious pecking order—the waitresses were from a local town and had been working there every summer since they were sixteen. They mostly ignored us. This was my very first lesson on inclusion—make your colleagues feel like they are a part of the team.

It wasn't great, but it was experience. Working hard will always beat out hardly working, IMO. My Fire Island restaurant experience has served me well over the years. Learn, grow, and move on up!

After graduating from college, I registered with a temp agency to start getting some office experience. My college summers had been spent in the previously mentioned restaurant and sleep-away-camp pursuits. My first temp job lasted maybe one day. I was to fill in for the receptionist. I was truly awful. The phone was one of those old-fashioned consoles with multiple lines lighting up. The horror! And there was that one red line. What *was* that? I was afraid of it. Needless to say, I was a *terrible* receptionist. Don't let anyone ever tell you it's an easy job—it's not. I moved on.

The next job was right up my alley. It must have been some kind of PR firm. They showed me to a room stacked high with boxes of paper. I was to create packets with the various different pages. Hundreds of them. But I was well suited to collating. In fact, you might say I was a collating dynamo. It ended up being a multiday job. They sent another young temp in to help me, but she didn't last. I'm confident she was intimidated by my speed with the stapler. I didn't know it at the time, but this job in particular prepared me well for my first "real" job as a legal assistant in a big NYC law firm.

I supplemented my income as a salesperson at Carroll Reed, a clothing store in my local mall geared toward middle-aged women in Fairfield County and the like. The Gap was paying $6 an hour, but Carroll Reed was $6.25. The choice was obvious. The hours were long, and my feet hurt like the dickens at the end of a shift. If nothing else, I was inspired to kick my job search into gear, and I did land one a few months later that would set me on my career path.

I think back to those days and the simplicity of it all. I am thankful to have experienced some "everyday jobs" and to have gained an appreciation for the people who are in those roles. I think it made me a better manager—the kind who at least tries to understand. And maybe a better human (I hope).

I spoke with a close friend recently, and we were reflecting on our careers. As I relayed my experience, it occurred to me just how opportunistic I have been. Job A led directly to Job B, and Job B led to Job C, and so forth. But it didn't happen in a reactionary way—my eyes were wide open, and I always had an updated résumé.

One weekend as I was installing Mortite around the window AC units at our vacation rental property while my husband looked at me quizzically (he grew up with central AC), I had a thought. I recalled that this had been my job at the beginning of every summer during my childhood when my dad had gone around the house installing ACs in the bedrooms. I had dutifully followed right behind him with the Mortite for our drafty old windows. I won a lot of points with my husband when I pulled out the Mortite many years later to solve our leaky-window problem—he thought I was a genius.

I sometimes wonder if the universe places experiences strategically in our paths to prepare us for the next experience, and so forth. Because when I look back, hindsight truly is twenty-twenty, and the progression seems obvious. Which begs the question, Can we predict the future by looking at the past and present? Do we even want to? If I knew the first time I had a tough experience that it would be replaced with a tougher experience that would eventually give way to an even tougher experience, would I have followed through? Probably.

Maybe life is just about laying groundwork, building a foundation, and then adding on. Whatever it is, the past does inform the future. So pay attention!

» Keep Looking Forward

I work in NYC, and as I ran down Fifth Avenue in heels one day (hoping not to be late to my next meeting), I thought about another time, a number of years ago, when I had been running *up* Fifth Avenue in heels.

That morning, I had been on my way to a very important interview—hoping to win the coveted spot of summer associate at JLL. It had been raining, and the subways had been delayed, so I'd been late. In my young mind, I'd thought, "Is the rain meant to deter me? Am I late because I am not 'supposed to' get this job?" I'd landed the job, but over the years, the emotions of that day have revisited me.

As I ran (yet again!), I realized the message was this: My career will keep me running. It will always push me forward. There will be obstacles (have you seen the crowds on Fifth Avenue?), and there will be circumstances beyond my control (rain, subways). There will be a fast pace, and I will be forever busy (running from meeting to meeting).

The good news is the rain did *not* deter me, and I *was* "supposed to" get the job. I have enjoyed a collective fifteen-plus years with this same company and have benefitted greatly while making a tangible impact. So I will continue to run around NYC—jumping from meeting to meeting—but maybe I will switch to sneakers.

One day, I saw a guy in his fifties wearing his high school football jacket at the bagel store. Where I live, there is a serious football rivalry between two neighboring towns, and many of the men who have participated constantly hearken back to the "glory days" and their memories of "The Game" from the 1970s, '80s, etc.—you get the point. It is bittersweet for them, no doubt, as they must have loved the team spirit, the brotherhood. And oh, the wins! But oh, the losses!

While there is something romantic about the glory days, we can also feel tethered to (and therefore stuck in) that time long ago when we were young and had not a care in the world. But spending too much time in the past can limit opportunities for the future. When looking back, I focus on how my experiences and relationships helped build my future. I can say with full confidence I am completely and always focused on the road ahead—always trying to understand the best path to achieving my goals.

Hopefully your own glory-days memories don't keep you overly tied to the past. Finding a way to use those exciting experiences to influence your future performance is a productive way to break free. If you loved winning then, keep pursuing the wins now, and don't let any touchdown be your last!

» **Be Open to Your Next Opportunity**

There is a career runway in front of you, but can you see it? I mean really see it? Perhaps not! So you had better take flight soon!

In 2018, I announced to my team I was leaving after five-plus great years to pursue a new opportunity with our company (that global account director role I mentioned earlier). My voice cracked, and the words had trouble flowing. It was surprising to me and many in the room. But the reason it happened is simple: love. I loved my team, and I loved my work. It reminded me of a saying I have seen on many Life is Good T-shirts: "Do what you love; love what you do." If you don't love what you are doing, then get yourself to something you do love! And go do it!

When my kids were little, my mother-in-law had a habit of warning them when something was going to be frightening or unnerving: "Don't be scared!" she would say. Of course, this would unleash instant panic, anxiety, alarms, tears . . . nothing like telling someone "You are about to be terrorized!"

In terms of career advancement, being scared is a really good thing. If you are not scared at your job at least a few times each week, you may want to consider stepping out of that cushy comfort zone. It's hard to do, especially as you get more comfortable. But being scared helps you test your limits and pushes you to grow your knowledge and skills. I am not talking about being scared of your boss or coworkers or safety hazards—those things you should try to fix or move on from. If you don't have a little fear in your day to day, get some. Good for the soul, I say.

On another note, some of the best opportunities I've had have come to me when I was not necessarily "ready." I meet regularly with my direct reports, and as soon as someone tells me they will be "ready" for their next role in a year or other period of time, that next role comes knocking on the door sooner than predicted. It never fails. We recently lost a team member to a competitor because we were grooming him to be "ready" for his next role. Well, guess what? The competitor thought he *was* ready and gave him the promotion (and the money, by the way) he had been driving for. Being *willing* and *able* is far more important than being *ready*, because opportunities don't wait for you to get your stuff in order. They are dropped in your lap and need to be acted upon, whether you are ready or not! I recently reached out to some colleagues for referrals—I had a role open that needed to be filled quickly. One of them contacted a potential candidate, and the résumé came forth almost instantaneously. Strike while the iron is hot, but more importantly, be ready to do so. Keep your résumé updated. Don't ever get caught flat-footed. It can happen, especially during a volatile economic period. But why not be prepared anyway? You never know when opportunity will come knocking.

Are you listening for it?

» Look Around for Hidden Mentors and Role Models

My elementary school lunch lady was Mrs. Falkenstein. We were literally petrified of her. She had a German accent and ran a very tight ship. When she said to line up, we lined up. When she said to sit down, we sat down. Once in a while, some brave soul would challenge her. This individual would be told very loudly they were "staying in" for recess, which meant they would spend their playground time with Mrs. Falkenstein. Yikes!

Mrs. Falkenstein was exceptionally strict. She could get hundreds of kids in an institutional environment to eat their lunch in a timely fashion, which could help them make it through the rest of the day. She processed us in an orderly way and didn't tolerate disruption. When challenged, she challenged back. She was intimidating but never out of line or mean. In a rare moment, someone would get her to crack a smile or laugh, and those were great days.

Mrs. Falkenstein approached her role with passion and tenacity. It's funny to now think back and realize she was one of my first female role models. Although it was a bit scary at the time, I am impressed at what a cool lady she was. She certainly faced some tough customers but overall had a strong impact on us—that is for sure!

One of the very first female role models I worked with was a senior partner in a prestigious law firm. She was a committed professional who sat at a desk in the World Trade Center behind multiple piles of papers—you sometimes couldn't see her when you walked into her office. (She was barely five feet tall.) She was a dynamic, savvy lawyer—a tiny woman with a brilliant mind and impeccable work ethic. She was generally pleasant. But guess what? People were slightly uncomfortable around her. I was fascinated by this because on paper, there was a lot to like about her: Ivy League credentials and a groundbreaking legal practice. But she didn't give off the warm fuzzies, and people were confused.

At the time I was way early in my career and had not really figured it all out yet (still haven't). I was considering two different paths: business or education. I thought about this lady and realized what a minority she was in the business/law field. It occurred to me that if I pursued a degree in business, I could have a greater impact—we needed more female leaders. So I applied to business school, and the rest is history.

Sometimes inspiration comes from very quiet corners—for sure this time it did, but I hope that is where the quiet ends. I will do my part . . .

» Give Yourself a Break

This one goes out to those considering heading back to the workforce after time doing other important things. It was 2010, and I had been home with my children since 2003. It had been a tough decision to give up half our income, but during those years, while experiencing the joy of all the girls' "firsts," I took every leadership or consulting opportunity that came my way. When the kids were both school age, it was my turn. I began to network and within six months was employed. My strategy was to dive back in full time, commute to NYC, and get promoted to VP in five years.

I threw myself back in. It was hard on the family for the first few months until I had proven myself and could negotiate Fridays at home. But I put my nose to the grindstone every day. Within the first four months, a colleague resigned, and I offered to absorb her workload if I could have a direct report. Suddenly my portfolio doubled, and within one and a half years, I was VP.

Today, more than eleven years later, I am an executive managing director running a $40 million business and directly leading a high-value team of 260 people. The point of this story? It is possible to restart your career and succeed. Define your priorities, set up a structure for support at home, and get to it. You can accomplish anything you want to with the right plan and people around you!

» **Keep the Faith**

When I was six months out of college with no job, this particular law firm rejected me. Somehow, I did not take no for an answer and contacted them again. It happened they were "desperate," as they had been appointed the underwriters' rep for the Resolution Trust Corporation, a government entity conducting the savings and loan bailout, a huge deal. Maybe they saw something in me and gave me the chance I needed. More likely they determined I had a pulse and could plug a hole—make copies and proofread documents in a semi-twenty-four-seven capacity. It doesn't really matter because the point is my timing was right. My résumé hit "someone's" desk when the desperation ensued, and they called me in. I met with the associate and the recruiter (whose job I would assume less than two years later). I was in! This led to my first management role, which encouraged me to apply to business school, where I was recruited by my current employer, and the rest is history.

So it *is* true: if at first you don't succeed, then try, try again. Also, believe that timing is everything and that eventually you will get the timing right. Gratitude to those who gave me that first break. And fortitude to those who are looking for theirs now!

» Stay in the Game

Even after I left the workforce in 2003, I spent the next eight years as a part-time consultant before reentering the workforce full time in 2010. To think, the reason I made the choice to exit the corporate world was because I did not have the opportunity to telecommute or work from home. My, how things have changed for the better. I now work from pretty much anywhere—a train, a car, an airport, a plane. I might have even worked from the beach a time or two (unconfirmed). I have run a videoconference call from the car while someone else was driving. I have battled stink bugs while on international calls. This all probably sounds like business as usual to many of you, especially after what we have been through during the COVID-19 crisis. It was not at all normal way back in 2003. I am glad we have progressed in this way—there is hope our children will have more rather than fewer opportunities than we did, and more parents will be able to flex their schedules and environs to be involved in their families' care.

One morning about eight years ago when I was driving my sixth grader to school, she turned to me and said, "Mom, does it get any easier?" What a tough question for a parent to answer, especially knowing the answer she wanted to hear was a resounding *yes*—but that wouldn't have been true.

"It doesn't get easier," I said, "but things change. You build strength and courage over time to face the hardships of life. The experiences you are having now will embolden you to face bigger challenges someday, and so forth." Heavy stuff for 7:45 a.m. on a Tuesday.

The other day I was meeting with a young rising star in my office, and we were discussing a similar topic—that some of the things we experience in our careers (relationships, disappointments, failures) are important for building strength, courage, and resolve. I told her I sometimes advise people "Don't work for a terrible boss" but have realized lately I learned some of my greatest lessons from those awful bosses. So maybe the advice should be that it's okay to sign up for something that is horrible; just don't do it long term.

In retrospect, the answer to my daughter's question really was *yes*, it does get easier. But it gets harder before it gets easier, and that's part of life. From where I sit now, the challenges are easier to address because I have the experience. It wasn't "easy" getting here, but it's been an interesting ride!

A close friend sends me a text every time he travels and his flight lands safely. "Roached." One word. He explained to me that he is a survivor—he has had sickness, been fired from jobs, lost everything, and then gained it back. None of it has dampened his spirits—in fact, quite the opposite: he is filled with resolve. He truly believes he could survive the apocalypse—just like the roaches will. I would say that at seventy-something years of age, he is the most ambitious person I know. He continues to dream and is currently chasing a billion-dollar business plan.

Too often we let our failures and losses set us back, sometimes further than they deserve. Most of us face adversity, whether in our public or private lives, and the key is to not back down. Keep going; keep pushing. Maybe if it's not working, you need to change your circumstances. Or do an end run around the blockers or climb right over them. Bulldoze through them if you have to!

They say what doesn't kill us makes us stronger. It's true. It's also true that I have killed my share of roaches in my life. But they keep coming back, don't they? Be someone's roach problem, and get your ideas heard, your promotion pushed through, your recognition achieved. And send me a "Roached" when you succeed!

» Go at Your Own Pace

The Tortoise and the Hare was one of my favorite stories growing up. I was always an endurance person, not a sprinter. In everything. Which I suppose is a main reason I found my way into real estate management.

My dad passed away in 2017. I was able to be with him, by his side that morning. The next day, I went for a walk on Lido Beach in Sarasota, Florida, a place where my family had vacationed many times during my childhood. I came upon a tiny sand sculpture of a sea turtle—close enough to a tortoise for me to think it was a sign from my dad. He had always been supportive of my career and excited when he saw my progress. He knew I had chosen a slower path for career growth. It was all good.

I think the key is to not think or worry about what others are doing but focus on your own path. It may take detours and go in circles, but as long as you are moving forward and learning, you will be a winner in the end. I'm so glad I ran into the little turtle that day. I needed a sign that I was on the right track. Ironically, my path went on a detour shortly after that experience but eventually led me to great things and amazing people. Maybe my dad had a hand?

» Make it Happen

When our children were young, friends came to visit with their little ones, and they marveled at the fact that our kids stayed in bed after good night kisses while theirs kept popping back up, asking for Chinese food, wanting attention, coming up with any and all excuses to not go to bed.

"You're *so* lucky!" they said to us. Luck nothing! That took painful training and lots of tough nights. It was purely the result of effort and dedication to ensure our children could soothe themselves to sleep.

It's the same with your career. A friend of mine who is an incredible mentor read me the riot act recently. "You aren't just *lucky* that you have experienced strong career growth. You talk as if the people who provided referrals for you won those jobs for you. They didn't. *You* did." He was right. I personally tend to think I am *lucky*. But it's not luck. Sure, those connections help a lot because they get you in front of the right people. But then, it is up to you to prove your worth, and if you get the job, *you* did it. And then if you excel at the job—well, that's *all* you.

So don't be like me and think you are *lucky*. I'd rather hear you say you were *plucky* and that you made it happen yourself. Because you did.

Don't worry if you feel lost. Keep your chin up, and know that there is hope for you if you keep your senses open. "If you only look around, you will be found"—a great lyric from *Dear Evan*

Hansen. Amazing inspiration in those few words. A simple concept but so true. You have to put your career desires out there. It's easy. Start by writing down what is important to you in the next job. Set goals in the words you use. Even lofty goals—why not? What do you really, *really* want?

I am living proof. I did this a couple of years ago following a mentoring session with a good friend. He told me, "Write down everything you want out of that next role." I wrote down some crazy stuff. Not kidding—the next day I got an email from someone recruiting for the absolute perfect next role for me (the role I am in today). Put some time aside, and set your goals. Then "send" them out to the universe. You *will* be found!

Build Your Network

In real estate we always say *location, location, location*. But in recruiting and job searches, connections rule the day! Can't stress it enough: ABC—Always Be Connecting. Your network is the number one most important tool in driving your career forward. People I met twenty-plus years ago and kept in my network are still influencing my career. That's the truth. In my role, I am hiring every day—and when someone comes to me with a referral, it makes my job much easier. A box checked. So ABC—Always Be Connecting—and move yourself onward and upward!

Someone on my team forwarded the résumé of an outstanding manager she had worked with some years ago. Her endorsement was glowing, to say the least. I met with the candidate, and we connected on multiple levels. Although I didn't have anything available at the time, we agreed to stay in touch.

Fast-forward a few months, and she reached out about a role she saw listed. I am good friends with the hiring manager, so I contacted her. Who would have known—these two already knew each other from previous roles almost ten years prior but had lost touch. They reconnected, and I am happy to say it was a match!

In 1997, I interviewed a young woman about my age for an assistant general manager position at JLL. I noticed halfway through the interview she was sitting there staring at me, mouth agape. I said, "What?"

And she said, "I have just never seen anyone so enthusiastic about their company. I am half expecting you to whip out some pom-poms and do a cheer." She was hired, and we worked together for a few years.

I left the company for a role in corporate real estate, and she left about two years later. She did a stint in residential real estate, and my husband was able to refer a few clients. I became a mom and decided to stay home for a few years. She connected me with a friend who worked for Liz Lange, and I did a maternity modeling gig on TV. The back-and-forth of our connectivity was simply crazy—but became less and less surprising. Ultimately, in 2009, she returned to JLL.

She called me out of the blue in 2010. "Hey—would you be interested in coming back to JLL? I think we have a role that would be perfect for you." Thinking about the pom-poms comment back in 1997, I went to Party City and made a purchase. I showed up to my interview with a set of pom-poms and gave them to her. We laughed, and I was eventually hired.

She left the company, gave me the pom-poms, and took a big global role somewhere else. Four years later, she decided to take some time off before finding her next adventure. We got together in 2019, and guess what? That's right—the pom-poms came out again because she was hired back to my team! That was certainly something to cheer about!

Here's to the mighty network, which frankly always bears fruit: get your résumé into the hands of people who can get it into the hands of *people who will hire you.*

» It's Never Too Late

In college I took a German literature course taught by a no-nonsense German gentleman. He had a great sense of humor, even though many of the books we read were heavy, taking place in Germany during the first half of the twentieth century. He was engaging, animated, and fun—it was a class you took for the professor rather than the subject.

Often, when Professor Arnold returned our papers, he would implore us to cut the BS. "If anyone ever finds a rubber stamp of a bull with a slash through it, please send it along. I need it!" For some reason that stuck with me, and whenever I was in a store that sold rubber stamps, I would look, but never with any success.

Years later, I met a fellow who told me he owned a company that manufactured, among other things, rubber stamps. Would you believe it? I told him the story about my professor. Within days, a package arrived in the mail—a rubber stamp of a bull with a slash through it. No bull! I quickly searched the internet to find my former prof, who was thankfully still associated with the college. I sent him an email. He wrote back, incredulous! And thankful. I sent him the stamp and closed the loop on a seventeen-year-old request. It is never too late to connect the dots!

You determine what you try next. A colleague who had been in his role for fifteen years came to me one day to tell me he was leaving. I asked, "Why?"

He said he was inspired by someone who had recently run for president of the United States. (I won't tell you who.) I gave him a puzzled look, and he said, "Hear me out." He went on to explain that he had considered staying where he was and "riding it out" to retirement. But he had seen this person of somewhat advanced age run for president—pursuing a new role and completely new adventure of profound proportions when many people envision themselves volunteering, playing golf, doing crossword puzzles, and such. He said if that person has the energy to pursue that job, then he himself should be able to try something new as well. Okay.

In April 2018, I attended a performance of *Hello, Dolly!* starring Bernadette Peters, age seventy. She commanded the stage and audience with true grace, immense charm, and stunning wit. I felt inspired and realized age should not be a barrier to furthering one's accomplishments. For me, age has brought wisdom and confidence—and it is good to know that others have been successful at continuing to grow their careers even as they move into the later stages of life!

Out in my garden, I thought my tomato plant was done producing, so I stopped watering it. And then one day a tiny red tomato showed up! Don't give up; new opportunities emerge every day, even when it seems like all bets are off. Keep pushing, and keep your eyes open. *Don't miss the new life growing on your vine!*

» Appreciate the Deep Connections

If looks could kill . . .

If you have seen *The Irishman*, you know the scene. Joe Pesci and Robert De Niro exchange looks while sitting across from each other in a restaurant, and although no words are spoken, the message is clear. A hit is being ordered.

Most of us, in our daily routines, are not ordering hits, thank goodness. But we are connecting with our colleagues in unspoken, subliminal ways that are a testament to the underlying trust and confidence we have built with each other. Those connections are *so* important to our success. And once you have established that kind of tie, it adds value to everything you do.

So look out for those highly connective relationships where the level of understanding transcends the obvious. They exist in a space we can't define but treasure every day. In my experience, these types of bonds last well beyond the trajectory of any particular job—it's chemistry, and it's real!

In seventh grade, I befriended a smart, wiry boy named Jordan in the hallway. It was literally a friendship "in passing" because I walked by his locker dozens of times each day in my travels. He always greeted me with a smile. At the tender age of twelve, he was honing his dry wit and would practice on me. So much fun—we were friends throughout high school.

He wrote in my seventh-grade yearbook, "Wherever you go, there you are." It's the only quote I have ever remembered from any of the many yearbooks I collected during my school years. Perhaps because I have been trying to figure out what it means to me, but it has been a refrain in my head for some forty years. (Yikes!)

It could mean there's no escaping who you really are. It could mean that all the baggage you collect over the years stays with you. It could mean that bringing your true self to every situation is a good thing. So many interpretations! So many years I have spent thinking about this!

It occurred to me that every time I think of it, I think of Jordan, who unfortunately left this earth too young when we were in our twenties. So whenever I recall this quote, there he is. Maybe it's not really about me—maybe the lesson is to bring a little piece of the great people you encounter in life with you wherever you go. Yes, that's what it means to me. What does it mean to you?

» Think Things Through

Talking points! A colleague of mine always gets his talking points together and plays them back to me and others before heading into difficult conversations. A very smart strategy. Sometimes going in cold can be a thrill or a test of your skills, but then again, who wants to take that risk in a business situation?

A friend of mine who doesn't follow sports told me whenever he has plans with other guys, he makes sure to read the sports pages that day so he is prepared to talk about the latest games. Genius! Being prepared can be a true enabler of success in any situation.

Recently, I had an experience where I could have used better talking points. As an adopted person, I have a hodgepodge family—some bio and some enviro. My half brother was visiting me for the first time ever, and we ran into someone I knew. I introduced him as my brother, without thinking about some of the potential ensuing questions that eventually did come. An example was, "So is it just the two of you, or are there more siblings?"

My awkward response amounted to "It's complicated" but was not nearly so eloquent. I might have thought to prepare talking points for the inevitable questions.

In the future, I plan to make it my business to be sure I have talking points for every situation—always!

» Connect with Humor

Laughter is a great way to connect with people. I recently reached a milestone with a colleague when, for the first time, we spent more than 50 percent of a one-on-one business call laughing. Some might say that was not a productive use of our time. However, in an industry that depends largely on relationship building, I saw that connection between us as a huge breakthrough.

Early in my career, I had a fantastic boss who took fifteen minutes every day to come out into the corridor and chat with the team. He would crack some jokes and always inspired belly laughs among us. It was a vital part of ensuring our team stayed connected.

Reaching that milestone with my colleague made me feel great. It opened the door to stronger connections and gave me confidence that we will build an outstanding partnership (and friendship, I hope). That will certainly help when the non-funny stuff happens. And the non-funny stuff is guaranteed to take place in a people-oriented business!

Humor is a critical tool in our relationship bag of tricks. Laughter is a unifying experience. I would go so far as to say that there are different levels of laughter, like those video games where you must achieve higher levels to open new doors and adventures. As you can imagine, full-blown belly laughter with tears is the highest level. The kind of laughter where you have to excuse yourself from class or a conference call. Those levels are rare, and those friendships—even rarer.

With some people, you can't get past the first level. But I am often able to sniff them out, abandoning wit and bringing in a little slapstick that anyone can appreciate. It doesn't always work, but mostly it does. I once had a boss who was so humorless that, to this day, I don't know if he has teeth because he never smiled!

There is a rush when you make it to a new level with a friend, a colleague, or even your boss. When you share a good laugh over something, whether personal or pertaining to work, the levels get higher and promote stronger ties—ties that bind. Humor adds levity, and levity breaks down barriers. It helps us relax and be more authentic, building confidence and friendship along the way!

» Be the Bridge

Heard about a friend who was going to work for a competitor, and I immediately reached out with congratulations. I mean, why not? This person had been a force in my career and was always good to me. I knew he had been seeking an opportunity like the one he'd found, and I was truly happy for him. One thing is for sure—the commercial real estate industry is a small world, and we all end up crossing paths over and over again. Anyone who doesn't get that will not go very far!

The competition is fierce. They say to keep your friends close and your enemies closer. But the competition in my industry is more likely to be your future employer or colleagues than actual enemies. Something I noticed during the COVID-19 pandemic was that we all connected and came together very quickly to determine best practices and ensure everyone was safe. We reached across company lines to confirm and reconfirm that what we were doing was right and working. That collaboration saved time, money, and probably lives.

So keep your perspective big picture when it comes to trashing the competition. You never know who's listening, and you never know who will be picking up your paycheck someday!

» Keep in Touch

Remember that AT&T jingle "Reach out and touch someone"? That jingle itself probably wouldn't fly these days, but the sentiment still "rings" (sorry) true—it is important to stay in touch. I think about it often when I randomly hear from friends or colleagues who are just reaching out to check in. Recently I was lucky enough to visit with former colleagues in two different circumstances. How happy I was to receive the bear hugs, kisses, and general great vibes that went along with those interactions. I think about my former teams constantly, wondering how they are doing and feeling grateful for the time we spent together.

I also recently received a "reach out" from an esteemed colleague who thought I needed a boost. This person took time out of what I know was an extremely busy day to call and give me a shot of encouragement that I didn't even know I needed. I may keep that message forever.

Two former colleagues reached out to me over the holidays, ostensibly to just say hi and Happy Thanksgiving, but the real message was clear: "I miss you." In our daily travels, we come across many great people. They make an impression on us, and it sticks. Through the years, we get the good fortune to work with many of these smart, interesting individuals. But eventually someone needs to move on—to grow their career, get a new experience, or accommodate a personal circumstance. It is tough to let go.

When people reach out to reconnect, a new energy emerges. I felt a spring in my step after hearing from these two admired friends. I learned that they still think of me and have fond memories of our time working together. They brought messages of encouragement and support, which were welcome and reciprocated.

Today, even if you are swamped with work, headaches, or problems, reach out. There is someone out there who needs to hear from you. And who knows? You might just make your own day!

Find the Balance

When I met my husband, I was twenty-eight. I had decided, or accepted, that I might be single for the rest of my life. There was no particular reason for me to believe that other than that a number of my friends had started pairing off, and while I was kind of interested, I kind of wasn't. My focus was on getting it right at work—building a successful career so I could be independent if need be.

And then there he was. He showed up unannounced in my email inbox a few days after I sent a letter to my high school classmates inviting them to our ten-year reunion. "Hi, Caroline. This is Frank Gadaleta. How are you? I received your letter about the reunion and wanted to offer my help." Yeah. Right. I knew it was not true because he had not even shown up at the five-year reunion. But after some emails back and forth, we agreed to meet, and the rest, as they say, is history.

A couple of months into the relationship, I had an interesting dream. He and I were at a baseball game at the local recreation center where we had grown up. We were sitting on a little hill watching the game. A cute little family all holding hands walked over. But it wasn't just any family. It was *my* family. My parents and a smaller version of me and my brother. They walked over, looked at us, and smiled. We smiled back. They walked on. My understanding of this dream was that it was my childhood self saying it was okay for me to grow up and be with Frank. And in a way, I was letting go of childhood me. I knew when I woke up that Frank was the one. From then on, we began building our life together!

From day one of our relationship, it has been a true partnership—a give-and-take as we try to balance our needs and those of our children, extended families, and careers. For a while, I stayed home to take care of the children before they were school age. When I went back to work, we divided up responsibilities I had previously borne at home. After my first two years back at work, one of us was always working in the suburbs and relatively close to home. This made the school events and emergencies accessible to us. The point is we both helped. Sometimes it's not a spouse but a sibling or a grandparent who is there to pitch in and add to the balance. Sometimes it is an army of friends and/or relatives. The key is to accept that life is about building partnerships and that no one is truly successful on their very own.

Health and wellness are key factors too. On #worldmentalhealthday2020, I was reminded of a wonderful piece of advice I received from a friend during my freshman year of college. He said regular exercise was a critical contributor to providing balance and promoting focus in his life. He said exercise enabled him to be more efficient and organized with his schoolwork. I think about that advice often and have even shared it with friends and family when they have been struggling with stress, focus, etc. Nothing like working up a sweat or even just taking a nature walk to put you in a better frame of mind and give you time to think things through.

I spoke to my friend for the first time in a few years recently and told him this story. He had no recollection and in fact said he needs to exercise more! He was extremely surprised at his eighteen-year-old self. Incredulous, actually. I made sure he knew that he'd made a difference in my life and that I have carried his words with me for thirty-plus years.

A colleague shared an idea at a recent team meeting: "Don't check your email first thing in the morning." Good advice, because aren't we tempted to do so, and don't we (mostly) regret it?

I tried it and then came up with my own idea: "Put work away at a designated time each evening." It doesn't have to be the same time every night, but the point is to put it down! Walk away. Leave it for tomorrow. Somewhere along the line, we forgot there is more to life than electronic communications.

Employing these tactics was eye opening for me. I think sometimes we forget how much we let electronics dominate our lives. Many of my peers are focused on limiting their teenagers' screen time. But what about ours? Practice what you preach, put the phone away, and do something that makes you happy instead!

Dare to Dream

I was on a call with a friend and colleague, and she said, "I am working so much I don't have time to dream." *What?*

I'm sure you have heard the old saying "If you're not growing, you're dying." Well, I would go a step further and say, "If you're not dreaming, you're just asleep!" Dreams give us goals, and goals help define a path, and a path makes things so much less daunting and scary. Without dreams, would we have only nightmares? No, of course not, but some of the color in our lives would surely fade.

Make time for dreaming. Think about what else is ahead. Dream a little dream. And don't just sleep through life!

When my daughter left for college, I wrote her a note in which I asked her to promise she would always follow her North Star—the light that guides her toward her dreams. I wrote that along the way as she journeyed through life, her North Star might change, and that's okay. No, that's *great* because it means she is achieving her dreams and creating new ones!

A friend of mine in high school had a tagline for whenever one of us stated "I hope XYZ" or "I wish ABC." She would say, "Dare to dream!" It was sarcasm, but let's put that aside. Dreams are important. They help us create goals. They give us hope and inspiration. Should you dream with a grain of salt? Sure, if it makes you feel better. But dreams propel us forward in our lives and drive us to *build* our lives rather than just *live*.

Langston Hughes wrote, "Hold fast to dreams."

Martin Luther King Jr. said, "I have a dream."

Dreams aren't just for sleeping—they light up our North Stars that guide us to our destinies. Will you dare to dream?

The benches at my local beach have all been donated by families and dedicated to their dear departed loved ones. One such bench has stood out to me for many years. The inscription reads, "When people say dreams don't come true, tell them about Rudy J. Colaluca." Who was Rudy? I have wondered over the years. And what did he dream of?

I had always pictured Rudy to be an older man who died living his version of the dream—surrounded by grandchildren, operating his own business, enjoying walks on the beach—but when I decided to research him, I found that could not have been further from the truth. He passed at the tender age of twenty-three. And yet his family thought of him as someone whose dreams had come true or someone who had helped others bring their dreams to life. How, at such a young age? The message is clear: It's not about how much time you have. It is about using the time you have to make your dreams come true.

It is never too late to pursue a new dream. Thanks to his family, Rudy J. Colaluca is still inspiring dreamers thirty years after he left the earth. Strangers who never knew him, even. Maybe that was Rudy's dream—to keep the spirit of dreaming alive. If that is true, what an amazing legacy!

Use Your Senses

A priest was in his church during a terrible rainstorm, and the floodwaters began to rise. He stood on one of the pews to avoid the water. A policeman came by and said, "Father, come with me! I will save you from these floods."

The priest said, "Thank you, my son, but God will save me." The policeman moved on, and the floodwaters rose. The priest climbed the stairs to the second floor.

A fireman came by with a hook and ladder and said, "Father, come with me. I will save you from these floods!"

"Thank you, my son, but God will save me." The fireman went on his way, and the floodwaters rose.

The priest climbed to the steeple, and a helicopter came by. The pilot yelled, "Father, come with me! I will save you from these floods!"

"Thank you, my son, but God will save me." The helicopter flew away, and shortly thereafter, the priest drowned.

When he arrived in heaven, he asked for a meeting with God. "Father, I believed you would save me!"

God replied, "I tried! I sent you the police, a fire truck, a helicopter . . ."

Not reading the signs that you are in a worsening situation is no laughing matter. Pay attention to the signs around you, and take advantage of the opportunities that come your way. Before it's too late! I was once in a role where my manager and his boss actively tried to undermine my career. It was devastating for me, especially as my client was supportive and actively trying to keep me engaged on the team. Ultimately I knew I had to find a new opportunity in a different company or business line. I read the signs and got out of there fast, before it was too late. The end result was that I found a more senior role with an incredible leadership team. But I had to proactively assess and change my situation—that was the key.

Sometimes it's just about trusting your instincts. How well do you trust your gut? I generally trust mine implicitly. Have I always listened to it? No! But over time, as a result of those mistakes, I have become acutely aware of the power of the *gut feeling*.

When my daughter was applying to colleges, I told her to wait for that feeling in her gut—the one that says "*Yes*, this is where I want to be for the next four years!" We visited a campus, and when the tour was over, we shared a collective sniffle (had to maintain decorum) in the bookstore because we agreed *this* was it.

It's the same with your career. If you have the good fortune to be choosy in your job search, you can get a good feeling about a particular role and a bad feeling about another. How amazing it is that the brain can take in certain data points, process them, and turn them into emotion. Of course, this happens with everything we do, so why not with career decisions? It is truly joyful when you get that positive vibe about a role—ecstatic excitement about the possibilities! So if you can, hold out for it. Go with the gut, and channel that positive energy into real success!

CHAPTER FOUR:
Manage with Finesse

Management is about building high-value teams. "It takes a leap of faith to get things going; it takes a leap of faith—you gotta show some guts." Bruce Springsteen makes it clear: taking risks has to do with intestinal fortitude. As a manager, I have taken some risks, especially when faced with hiring decisions. If a person is eager and excited to push themselves to take a big step forward, I am right there with them. Have I been burned? Sure. But frankly not that often. Typically, I have found people rise to the occasion. And when they don't, they step aside, and I take over until there is a replacement, but I can feel good knowing I took a chance and gave someone an opportunity. Never any regrets on that.

I have been the victim of people who didn't have the intestinal fortitude to give me a chance. I can't explain why, but sometimes chemistry (or lack thereof) overrides all else. And at those moments, we have to move on and accept that it wasn't meant to be. Still, I would continue to recommend the leap of faith. When it doesn't work out, it is surely upsetting. But when you see some-one rise to the occasion and become a star—well, that's worth just about everything and more.

Being an Effective Manager

Who was your best boss ever, and what were the characteristics that made him or her so? For me, the best have had the following going for them: sense of humor, experience, and sincere care for me as a person as well as my family. They also left me alone to do my work and provided support on an as-needed basis, ran interfer-ence with senior management, promoted me proactively without me having to beg, and had a very even temper with no sign of ego or need to blow their own horn. If anything, their priority was to push for recognition of their team within the organization. Take the time to think about how *you* define a great direct manager and how you can emulate those traits. Here are a few to think about:

» Flexibility

In my experience in the service business, clients have asked us to do the darnedest things. Sometimes those things have nothing to do with your scope, but you do them anyway to help build good will. Chances are, if you are asked to complete an outlandish task outside of your scope, it is because the client trusts you to get it done. That is *good* news. This is not scope creep—this is jumping in to help your partner perform something they are otherwise at a loss to complete.

Building good will is an important part of client-relationship management. Solving weird problems can help get you there. Being adaptable enough to help your client out of a pickle wins many points. And then, just when you think you have seen it all . . .

» **Situational Awareness**

I was adopted as a baby. Tuck that info away, and let me tell you a story.

I was chatting with someone about affluent single women who spend large sums of money to freeze their eggs and plan to potentially use a surrogate mother to carry their babies to term in the future. This person was amazed at the popularity of this practice—I was too, but I also get it. Then he said, "But, Caroline, how does a mother really love a baby if she doesn't carry it herself?"

Ugh. No. Not what you say to an adopted person or frankly anyone in the adoption triad. I brushed it off and said, "Well, it's hard to say . . ." and tried to explain about love for children coming from many different sources. He wasn't convinced, but the point is: know your audience. I can't tell you how many times I have made these types of flubs. Countless! It's so avoidable. Think a few steps ahead before making blanket statements, or simply don't make them at all! (I truly wish I would take my own advice.)

We all have biases and opinions and don't always know where the people we talk to are coming from. In a friendly situation, no big deal. But if you are talking to your boss, your team, or a coworker, it could have implications on your reputation and sphere of influence. Don't do it!

A funny story that comes to mind has to do with . . . sneeze etiquette. Yes, it's true. I worked in an office where there was a mix of employees from both the client's and the service provider's teams. One of the client's employees was prone to sneezing. My natural inclination in a sneeze scenario is to offer a blessing—God bless you. Not for religious reasons; I just always thought it was polite. This person—who, by the way, was someone I liked a lot—would only say thank you if the person blessing was from the client side. Bizarre, right? One of the client colleagues thought this was hysterical and would, on purpose, try to beat me to the punch, then wink at me when he got his thank-you. Well played.

To this day I don't think it was intentional—but if it was, that might be the weirdest microaggression I've ever heard about. Gesundheit!

Some days you won't be able to avoid controversy. A recent experience comes to mind. Every morning, I take my dog for a walk around our street. It is a perfect quarter-mile circle, and she is able to get all her "business" done in the time it takes to cover the entire block. On a typical day, we round the circle and are bombarded by at least one pair of vocal dogs who stay behind their Invisible Fence as they growl and bark at our mere existence.

But one day it was different. As we rounded the corner, I eyed the two offending Labradors and heard their voices beginning to bark at us. It starts with a growl and ends with a full-throated woof. I looked at my sweet Penny and said, "Nope. Not today. Let's go back the way we came." We turned on a dime and reverted back toward home. But wouldn't you know it—by that time another neighbor had let their yappy little Yorkie out in the yard, and he (the dog, not the owner) let loose his fury on us. Sigh.

Lesson learned. If the dogs are going to bark at you that day, they will find a way. You can try to circumvent but are better off facing their wrath, letting them get it off their chests, and then moving on. There is no need to avoid. After all, a bark today might save you from a bite tomorrow . . . you simply never know.

How Can You Grow as a Manager?

» Seek Out Trustworthy People

Never underestimate the importance of a great consigliere or right-hand man or woman. My favorite such character of all time has to be Silvio Dante from *The Sopranos*—partially because how cool was it to have a member of the E Street Band on *The Sopranos*? More importantly, this character was truly the heart and soul and everything in between when Tony needed him. I have had the sincere pleasure of playing this role for others as well as having this special person by my side when I've assumed various leadership positions over the years. I cannot stress enough the importance of having that dependable person by your side—to advise and support on a moment's notice. I have always owed and given credit for my success to those who stood next to me as my right-hand people. It was literally not possible without them.

In my current role, I have several of them. Each is driving the business forward with their clients and building the relationships that will help foster our growth. I am so grateful to have these strong leaders by my side as we wade through daily activities. And we might share some wine and a fine Italian meal here and there as well!

Building a team you can trust is critical to managerial success. The Radio City Rockettes are an amazing team. We go to the *Christmas Spectacular* each year and are awed every time. The piece that gets to me most is the "Parade of the Wooden Soldiers." The ladies' precision in keeping time with each other is, as usual, impeccable. As they fold into formation to perform various coordinated dances, I think about the business world, which is not always so perfectly choreographed but definitely requires collaboration with others to ensure a spectacular result.

At the end of the dance, the soldiers line up behind one another, and a toy cannon is brought out to deliver a *bang*. Here is where things get interesting. The front dancer begins to fall backward, putting her weight on the dancer behind. At the same time, the dancer behind is interlocking her elbows with the dancer in front. A third dancer behind all of this begins to support the back of the middle dancer so as to break the fall. That teamwork persists throughout the line of forty or so dancers to enable a slow-motion backward fall that ends in a domino-like effect of soldiers, one falling back on the next, with the final dancer falling on a neatly placed pillow. At the end, they all sit up simultaneously and salute the crowd. Bravo! A soft landing thanks to a well-integrated team!

» Celebrate Diversity

I managed a team that was 80 percent diverse, and I was often asked, "How do you do it?" The key to maximizing the impact of diversity is through inclusion. Every discussion panel has diverse representation; every team member has the opportunity to contribute to every team meeting; recognition is distributed evenly; every voice is asked to speak up. Inclusion is woven into the fabric of everything we do, and we have an award-winning team that achieves outstanding results. That is how we do it!

Do you remember the Enjoli perfume commercial from the 1970s and '80s? It featured an attractive woman wielding a frying pan, wearing a silky dress, and singing a jingle: "I can bring home the bacon, fry it up in a pan. And never, never let you forget you're a man! 'Cause I'm a woman—Enjoli!" I was obsessed with this commercial for some reason as a young girl. I periodically think about it when I am juggling the competing demands of my life. Fortunately, I do think things have progressed from the days of the Enjoli commercial, where the working woman's role at home was still defined as cooking and pleasing her husband. My husband might say those were the good old days. But that might not work out so well for him—just sayin'.

These days it's not just moms trying to do it all. Dads, siblings, aunts, uncles, grandparents, and friends are all pitching in. And I think that is good for everyone. Why should the burden fall on a single demographic? Families should have the choice to share their responsibilities, and the concepts of diversity and inclusion can apply to any situation. Diversity and inclusion are about expanding the universe of who does what. I have heard people say, "It's good for business." And it is good for families too!

I once heard someone refer to a difficult client as a *tough cookie*. Ugh. From the further description of this lady (and you know it was a lady because we would rarely if ever call a man a *tough cookie*), I think if she heard herself called a *tough cookie*, she would have "made mincemeat" out of the person who said it. As long as we are using food references, this type of stuff truly drives me *bananas*.

We have a hard time describing strong women in our society. They are either a bitch (ouch) or a tough cookie (aw, she's not so bad). Why can't they be a power broker or a force to be reckoned with and leave it at that? We have to somehow include their femininity when we describe them. She is a "smart lady." Why isn't she just *smart* or *sharp*?

Here is what I ask of you: When you are talking about female colleagues, please forget they are female. They are just *colleagues*. Same goes for anyone else from any non-white-male persuasion. I know it's not easy; I struggle with it too. We are conditioned to qualify people who are outside of the status quo.

Let's not single people out. We need to normalize inclusion, and we can do that by dropping descriptions that highlight our differences.

Diversity is always important. In my experience, diverse teams drive better decisions and outcomes than nondiverse ones, and this has been well documented in the business world. There is no excuse for not pursuing diversity on your team. Do you know what a *manel* is? It's a panel discussion where the panelists are all male. Man + panel = manel. Brilliant, right? Well, not really, when you think that half the population and half the workforce is female. What about the ladies, everyone? I bet they have something to say! Corporations and associations, you *can* do better! Invite a woman or two to sit on your panel. You will be *amazed* and possibly even *inspired*. Make it your policy: *No more manels!*

» Be Adaptable to Survive

As I walked through a Sears in Waterford, Connecticut, a few years ago and surveyed the bare shelves and "Store Closing—Everything

Must Go!" signage, I wondered, *What went wrong?* How could such an iconic brand that was the go-to for tools and appliances go the way of the dinosaur? My immediate thought was the executives gutted it and refused to adapt to the changing times. The lack of adaptability must have been a key to their failure.

Too often companies think, "We got this. We have been doing this for years, and we know what our customers want." With serious disruption happening in multiple industries (especially real estate and retail, both of which severely affect companies like Sears), you can't just think it won't affect you. It will. The question is, Will you be able to adapt and keep up? More importantly, how will you?

As I caught up on some reading about workplace transformation, I thought about a beautiful caterpillar that appeared on our parsley plant one day and then took up residence on our exterior wall to begin his metamorphosis. The process would be long and kind of ugly, frankly, but soon he would emerge as a beautiful butterfly! A Building Owners and Managers Association study showed a significant number of respondents to a survey stated they believed the COVID-19 crisis would be transformative to the workplace. Well, I would say yes, it has to be. We were forced into isolation and found new ways of working (almost immediately!), and now our eyes have been opened to the possibilities. I noticed when people began returning to the workplace that my company's corridors were filled with joyful reunions, questions, helpful guidance, and people doing what they love to do: working together in person.

Postpandemic, "poor-culture" workplaces may die, and that is not such a bad thing. But companies like mine, where culture promotes productivity and where people like each other and get along—those workplaces will be reimagined and revitalized over time. And most likely, they will emerge even brighter and more beautiful than ever, just like the caterpillar!

» **Connect at All Levels**

When my husband was in law school, many of the students lived off campus. One of the close-by towns was a popular spot for housing, and students were told to find out about available apartments by visiting the local shoe-repair shop. Apparently, the shoe-repair guy knew of all the available rentals in town and could connect tenants with the right landlords. Of course!

This story tells us two things:

1. Connecting with the right people is an important factor in getting what you need.

2. Frontline customer service people have all the important information!

Too often the front lines are not valued as highly as they should be. Yet the big revenue generators are extremely reliant on the relationships built by these folks with their customers. Always remember the value they are bringing to your business, and make sure you have the right personalities in those roles. Keep the lines of communication open with them as well—the intelligence they will bring you about your customers will be invaluable and critical to your success!

» **Embrace Integrity**

On Mother's Day, I was thinking about how things changed during my hiatus from the corporate world. Not in the world itself but in me. In 2003, I was a new mom and knew precious little. The first few months were pure "survival," and I had not yet actually experienced many of the feelings I would ultimately know as a mother.

When returning to my career in 2010, I had been in the parental trenches for eight-plus years and had changed as a person. I looked at my work through a different set of lenses, and when things went awry in the workplace, there was no turning a blind eye or walking away. Having two daughters inspired me to speak up, to make a difference so the working world they would inherit someday was better than I had found it.

A caring colleague once told me, "Speaking up is not a great way to climb the corporate ladder." That may be an unfortunate truth. But if it is true, I am not deterred. My duty to improve the corporate environment can be achieved from the lower rungs— no problem. It's the legacy I will leave for my daughters. And for yours. Sons, too, of course, as we can all benefit from the type of progress that promotes inclusion and equality!

» **Show Kindness**

Patrick Swayze had some good advice for his bouncers in the movie *Road House* when he told them to "Be nice . . . until it's time . . . to not be nice." Some people mistake *nice* for *weak* and will try to take advantage. It says a lot about their personal character when they do. It's simply a fact of life, and I'm sure we have all been disappointed by colleagues who have tried to work the system. In those situations, you may need to take the time to right the ship and get everyone back on board (or make them walk the plank if appropriate!). And then you can go back to being nice . . . until it's time . . . once again . . . to not be nice!

Someone who meant well said to me, "Don't be so nice. Don't bring people candy and such. They will take advantage of you." I thought about this advice because I think it is always good to carefully consider advice, especially when it comes from people who care.

But I remembered that I made a decision long ago to, simply said, be nice. Over the years, people have mistaken my kindness for weakness, and frankly that has not often worked out so well for them. I would rather be nice, and bring people candy, and support my team than find someone to yell at or ignore each day.

It turns out people appreciate kindness. I surprised some staff members with candy on Halloween and then again on Valentine's Day. Those employees aren't on my team anymore, as we have all moved on to bigger and better things. But guess what? They still remember and mention it every time I see them. I have a candy jar in my office at work, and it gets depleted at least once a week. And I get the benefit of conversations with the candy eaters who might not otherwise have stopped by!

» You Be You

A funny thing happened recently. I was interviewing a newly minted college grad, and she asked me a pointed question. "In an industry that is so male dominated, how do you make sure your voice is heard?" Very insightful question from someone just starting out, and good for her for thinking about those X factors she may face over the course of her career.

The question threw me a bit. I'm so used to working with men; it's not something I have had to address lately. So I had to think. And what I realized is this: In order to be heard, I inject something that is uniquely me into the conversation. For me, that's humor. Typically, sarcasm, to be precise. You can always count on a quip from my corner. It's my way of getting their attention. It also cuts the tension. And then they know I am in the room.

I told this young woman that not everyone thinks I am funny. In fact, I have escaped some pretty terrible managers who couldn't laugh with me. But my best colleagues could see the humor and sometimes the ridiculousness in parts of our business, and that made all the difference.

You've heard people say, "Bring your authentic self." I couldn't agree more. Bring what is unique to you; show how you stand out. They will know you are in the room, and they will hear you—loud and clear!

» Reward Passion

The other day I had the pleasure of taking the trash tour at Grand Central Terminal. I bet you never knew such a thing existed! (It doesn't, by the way.) But when your company manages a portion of the building for the Metropolitan Transportation Authority, let's just say there are "perks" you don't get elsewhere.

We were touring to help us understand the logistics of trash in a multiuse transportation facility. If you look at the infrastructure of Grand Central, you can figure out pretty quickly that it was not designed to hold a multitude of restaurants and quick-service food stalls, but for the modern traveler, those amenities are critical. So the team at GCT makes do with what they have.

Hauling trash at GCT is what I would call a logistics problem—lots of people, lots of trash, minimal staging areas, and difficult access to the compactor (an elevator ride away). It was clear the team works tirelessly to make trash go away.

My team showed up incredibly well—the pride in their jobs radiated from them. We saw a lot, but they wanted to show us more! We were tired and had to leave—it was five o'clock somewhere. They left an impression on me. I now see trash hauling as an important customer service area they strive hard to complete with the highest level of care. Impressive, to say the least. Inspired!

And then the other day my daughter had a college interview for a school she really loves. She said to me beforehand, "Mom, how do I prepare?"

I said, "Steer the conversation toward things you are passionate about."

After the interview, she said, "Mom, it went really well!" Points for Mom.

Another time I was interviewing for a role, and I was telling a colleague about it. She said to me, "You sound miserable!" She was correct—it wasn't the right role for me (and I didn't get it anyway). Phew!

Passion is important. You have seen people in action who are passionate about their work. Does it make you jealous? If so, maybe it's time to start thinking about a move. It's okay to step outside your box—the world will not fall apart. And happiness is contagious; you might just improve the lives of those around you as well!

» **Focus on Health and Wellness**

These days, many companies are laser focused on health and safety. Good news! But with the good always comes the flip side, unfortunately. One morning I arrived at work to find my colleague's son had been in an accident the day before. He was working for a scaffolding company, and a piece of equipment not properly secured had hit him in the face and hands while he'd been on the rig. He had been rushed to the hospital and received lots of stitches (no broken bones, thankfully) and bandages on his hands, and he would be unable to work for at least a week.

It turned out there were supposed to be three people on the rig, but there had been only two. That's pretty bad and most likely a root cause of the accident. Another root cause is likely that the staff had not been properly trained in safety protocols to secure the work area in the first place. But the worst parts of this entire story are that (a) they dropped the injured employee at the hospital alone with no escort, and (b) no family members were called. His mother found out via someone who'd heard about it. Say what? Come on, guys!

Safety protocols must be defined, trained, tested, and followed. Prevention is important, as is closing the communications loop. Follow up with root-cause analysis, and you are back at prevention. Easy. (Should be!)

One day I had a Big Mac attack at Chicago O'Hare. Don't ask. The young lady who served me was quite pleasant, and I remember thinking, "Very professional." A few hours later, I was in the ladies' room and heard sobbing. I saw that the same young lady was standing against the wall, hands to her face, crying her eyes out. Her manager was with her, consoling her, bringing her tissues, and holding her intermittently.

A random concerned traveler asked, "Is she going to be okay?"

The manager said, "She had a death in the family."

I said, "I'm so sorry," on my way out.

The whole scene brought tears to my own eyes, and upon reflection, I realized that is the job of a people manager: to take care of her people. So often managers subordinate their employees' needs, and then guess what happens? They don't have to worry about those employees anymore because they lose them!

Goodness help me if I ever neglect my people in favor of the business. That McDonald's team was undoubtedly stretched for a few minutes while the young lady composed herself. But so what? Having been well cared for, she would return to her post and get her job done professionally as she had before—and I bet with greater loyalty to her manager.

I was reading a book written specifically for women to tell them to "toughen up" and not be so *nice* when trying to build their careers (a recurring theme!). It basically told me all the things I was doing wrong and why I would never get ahead without changing my ways. Specifically, it said I should not mother people at work. Okay.

And then one day, I got an urgent call that one of my handymen had fallen off a ladder during a seizure and hit his head. He was bleeding and needed to go to the hospital. I dropped everything and ran through the streets of New York to get to the building. I arrived simultaneously with the paramedics, and he would not go with them. I was able to convince him to go and rode with him to the hospital. I sat with him until they were able to locate his wife. The truth is he almost died.

The incident scared him into turning his life around, and he became a new and much healthier man. He told me I was like a mother to him that day. By the way, he is only seven years younger than me. His statement certainly made me chuckle.

Needless to say, that book is in the garbage. I will manage my way and be who I am so my employees can be their best selves. Period and end of story!

What Challenges Does a Manager Face?

» Getting it Right with Recruiting

Recruiting is one of the toughest jobs a manager has. It is in no way an exact science, and it is quite frankly next to impossible to match all the relevant factors to exactly what you need. Think about it—a résumé is a summary of what a person has achieved. But there is no chemistry or sense of humor or disposition contained therein. And how does a person's potential really come through in a list of stats? Managers have to dig deeper.

When I took over my current role two years ago, my predecessor handed me a stack of résumés for candidates she had interviewed but not yet been able to place. I proceeded to follow up with the prospects to introduce myself. One of them stood out to me—it turns out he was a cancer survivor who had taken a hiatus from the workforce to take care of himself and then his mother. He had beaten a very deadly form of cancer, then spent time raising money for the cause, including a very impactful trip to Patagonia. I thought, "I must get this man on my team." He was clearly a resilient warrior, having defeated one of life's greatest and most inevitable challenges—death. Interestingly, he had also worked at some of the toughest real estate organizations in NYC (with some of the most feared and notorious characters). And survived. It took almost a year, but I eventually found the perfect role for him, and he joined!

Unfortunately, sometimes we can't tell a person's true potential from their résumé. My favorite part of Tom Brady's overall story is his draft pick. He basically almost didn't get hired for the job in which many people see him as being the greatest of all time. I can see how someone with his mindset would have been extremely motivated by that vote of so little confidence. I mean, look, being a part of the NFL draft means something and is not to be minimized, but I'm sure it was still tough to accept. Even though I am not a Pats fan, I am happy he was able to flip the script. Motivation can come from all sorts of places, and I love to see it bear fruit.

Who can truly predict success in a society with so many variables? If you study success, you'll find it's largely due to a confluence of circumstances that create an ideal situation. Hard work is often the control, not the variable. Chances are someone like Tom Brady would have been a winner no matter what because of his motivation and focus, but what if?

How do we as managers find the Tom Bradys in our midst? To me the key is understanding that there is more to a person than their résumé. When I interview, I look for a fire. There has to be something driving what's happening on paper. Tom Brady's story makes me realize I need to dig deeper when hiring and mentoring my team. Have you thought about what motivates you?

A few years into my career hiatus, I had the opportunity to interview for a real estate role at a large multinational media and technology company. The role was similar to the job I had left behind—my qualifications were not in question. But it went to a more junior person. They were worried I would get *bored*. They didn't understand that I was looking for a company to bring me back into the corporate world, not a fast career trajectory. I knew that if I found a firm where I could balance the demands of my life, I would happily embrace boredom in exchange for being back in the game.

Two years later, the phone rang. It was them. The person they had hired was moving on to a new role—she had used the experience as a stepping stone to her next move. They acknowledged, "We made a mistake." I politely declined to interview again.

The moral of this story is for hiring managers: The résumés of people who have taken time off to care for family or for other personal reasons will cross your desk. Give them a chance. When you do, you will earn their loyalty. The company that ultimately gave me that chance has earned mine—and gave me a fast career trajectory to boot!

» Knowing When to Promote

"Once you do *this*, then you'll be ready for *that*." It is a common refrain among managers when discussing career ambitions. But if an employee comes to you saying they are thinking about their next role, they are really saying, "Put me in, Coach! I'm ready to play *today*! Not next year or the year after. *Now!*" Keeping employees in roles they are good at just to plug holes is risky business. Ambitious professionals like to keep moving forward. Having the courage to push them onward and upward is smart.

I have learned the hard way; you have to listen to your employees to really understand when they are *ready*. They will tell you—either by saying "I am ready" or by leaving your organization if you don't help advance them. Losing great people costs money, so open your eyes and ears, and push your people to challenge themselves with new and different assignments. Throughout my career, I have mostly erred on the side of pushing people to their limits. It hasn't always ended well, but I never regretted giving it a try. Holding people back is in no way satisfying.

» Building a Cohesive Team

In a quiet moment, I was thinking back to my days as a camp counselor. On arrival day, hundreds of children would start a new adventure with a group of strangers around their age. Lots of awkward introductions ensued.

After dinner, we would bring each unit (forty-two campers) together for icebreakers. We sat in a huge circle in the rec hall and asked them to follow the lead of the counselor in the middle. The first activity was called Rain. The leader started by rubbing together the fingertips of each of her hands. She would slowly have everyone join: rubbing their hands together, then snapping, then clapping, then slapping their knees, then slapping the floor, then stomping their feet. If you closed your eyes, you heard the beauty of a torrential rainstorm all around you. Then slowly, she would direct the group to reverse the movements, until the storm was completely over. Everyone would clap, overwhelmed with joy.

What better way to build a team than by creating something beautiful together? That activity set the tone for the summer every time and got a group of strangers working together without their even knowing it. Surprisingly brilliant. After all, we were just a bunch of clueless college kids. Or were we?

The COVID-19 crisis was one of the greatest challenges I have ever faced in my career. I started a new role as tri-state head of property management in December 2019. By March 2020, my new team and I had been thrown into a new dimension we had never experienced before: dealing with a pandemic as we tried to safely manage our properties across the tri-state region. Our team worked on-site—embedded in their properties—and we unfortunately had not traditionally had many opportunities to interact on a personal level. But suddenly, there we were, connecting on a daily basis through video calls and constantly touching base. We even set up happy hour every week! If the pandemic had never taken place, the closeness we achieved as a team would have taken years—if it ever materialized at all.

And there was an added benefit I discovered. Crises bring forth strengths, and the many talents and capabilities of my team were revealed at warp speed. It's like I could see them through a microscope—so cool! We hit our stride as a team, and we could face anything. We were tested again when NYC was hit hard with looting and vandalism, shamefully eclipsing the extremely critical focus of the Black Lives Matter/George Floyd protests. But we carried on. I am tempted to ask the universe, "What else ya got for us?" I won't; we're good over here—plenty to keep us busy, thank you. But I sure am feeling lucky and proud!

» **Providing Motivational Feedback**

One of my most and least favorite seasons: annual reviews. Most, because I get to have a one-on-one with each of my direct reports to discuss my passion: them and their future. Least, because companies are still using biased "ratings" systems to categorize employees' performances. Ugh. Thankfully most companies abandoned these practices long ago, but some still hang on. It's troubling to me, especially when employees who get a certain rating that is considered *good* feel disappointed and discouraged. Was it worth it? I don't think so.

Another approach would be one I had heard from a previous client. Write down three areas of achievement from the year and three areas of improvement. Bam! Of course, if you had more kudos, you could give them, and the areas of improvement could spark a constructive conversation about what to do differently in the coming year. Sounds productive and positive to me!

I believe strongly that employers should abandon all numeric and otherwise highly subjective and therefore impossible-to-validate metrics used to measure human performance. Many companies have already done so, but these types of performance measurements are perfect playgrounds for manager biases, which is something we should never encourage.

A motivated employee who thinks they are a 4 out of 5 but gets rated a 3 suddenly questions whether they are valued as much as they thought they were. Isn't it better to give that person an opportunity to converse with their manager on what is working and what is not and make a plan for continued or improved success? I hope companies who rate employees discontinue this practice in the future. Subjective ratings are rife with bias and create breeding grounds for retaliation. Let's make more positive, constructive processes the norm and get people's careers and ambitions moving in the right direction. Who's with me?

» Managing the Pressure

Consider this my ode to the release valve. When things get heated, managers and leaders can do their employees a huge favor by taking a step back and easing the pressure. Having the confidence to give someone a little more time on a project, even if there could be heat from a client, or allowing someone to take a mental-health day to gather themselves, or even telling someone who is under the gun, "Don't worry; we've got your back"—that's leadership. These are powerful messages that not only release the steam but also help build trust and loyalty. Interestingly, those who manage with a heavier hand seem to expect the most loyalty but fail and then are surprised when employees leave them. *And* they hold a grudge. Seriously?

A message like "I support you/I agree with you 100 percent" goes such a long way! Another message I heard from a leader (just when I needed it, by the way) was equally powerful: "You win some; you lose some." The second part of the message was that it's okay to lose as long as you are winning more than losing. Makes sense! And releases a bit of steam.

Everyone needs a break. The pure stress of simply living in our world right now needs consideration. Let's use that release valve. Before the pressure prevails!

» **Meeting the Customers' Needs and Beyond**

If you're in a customer-facing industry, then you're familiar with the many challenges that come along with such a career.

The customer experience is alive and well a few miles down the road from me. Most New Yorkers have heard of Arthur Avenue, a.k.a. Little Italy in the Bronx. We recently made our first journey there to do some shopping. Thankfully, experienced friends and family guided us toward their favorite spots. It was an experience like no other. And it was all about how we were treated and the care with which our purchases were prepared.

We set out to buy pasta, meat, bread, and pastry. We realized quickly we had truly entered a little slice of Italy twenty minutes from our home. The friendliest, most helpful shopkeepers greeted us with amazing and vast delicacies. We requested meatball mix at the butcher—so what did they do? Ground it to order! At another store, we asked for two pounds of chicken cutlets—carefully sliced right in front of us. You need two pounds of fresh linguini (size number three!)? Here, let me prepare that for you right now. Cannolis are on the menu? Sure—I will fill them while you wait. Nothing fresher exists in the world. We would eat like kings and queens that evening!

We left that day with a renewed sense of excitement about retail shopping (and some fresh cannolis!). Businesses that can differentiate themselves with service and care will thrive. And keep people coming back for more!

Taking care of customers/clients is key to building and sustaining any business. Managers must be sure to build high-performing teams to ensure delivery of a quality product or service. Continuing on the food theme, I am reminded of my favorite deli—a family-owned enterprise where people line up by the dozens to order their favorite delicacies. A friend of mine uses the term *lunch meat* to describe unappealing, blah people. But it is also an unappetizing term for "cold cuts," which are an important staple of many American households. Most food shoppers will find themselves at the deli counter on a fairly regular basis. As I stood in line the other day, I saw that "the one," *the* deli man, was finishing up with a customer two heads in front of me. One should never underestimate the value of a great deli professional. I secretly hoped the timing would be right so he could assist me. The reason I covet his handiwork? He slices to perfection and delivers the selections in a neat and tidy way, always getting the order just right—and with a friendly greeting. The sandwich tastes better every time as a result.

That's what great service delivery is about, isn't it? Friendliness, efficiency, focusing on delivering a quality product that is satisfying to the customer . . . something as simple as slicing cold cuts gets messed up all the time—so much so that we may look down on them with disdain. As professionals, we don't want our work product to be lunch meat; we want it to be highly valued, even put on a pedestal at times. Fine delicacies, delivered to our clients with care!

» Differentiating Through Excellence

I saw a business called You Name It We Do It. How fun would it be to lob crazy requests their way to see if they can live up to their name? One-stop shopping has great value in our culture—the most obvious example being Amazon. In service delivery, it is more difficult to be a one-stop shop because it requires multiple skill sets, and most people are not jacks-of-all-trades. So we have come up with businesses to aggregate services.

One of the best business models is, quite frankly, the funeral home. They are a one-stop shop for all your memorial needs. They serve many functions—moral support, pallbearer, limo driver, and help with the church service. They do it all! At my father-in-law's memorial, the funeral director, Vinny, stepped in to walk my mother-in-law to her seat. Due to the soloist being late, we stood in the narthex, waiting to begin, for about fifteen minutes.

My husband leaned over and whispered to his mom, "Does Vinny know we want to drive Dad by the house?"

Vinny whispered back, "I do now!"

By the time we exited the church an hour later, a police escort was waiting to enable the home drive-by. Talk about getting things done quickly! So we will see if You Name It We Do It can survive. I hope they can, but they had better connect with the right people and the right skill sets—and fast!

A restaurant in my neighborhood caters beautifully to elderly people. On a recent visit (they also cater to Groupon members), I was mesmerized by the level of care given to a multitude of quite frail customers. The owner (who lives walking distance from his restaurant) has engaged an army of gentle soldiers to attend to the needs of their aging clientele: assisting with walkers, pulling out tables, offering a hand or an arm (or several) to help people to their seats.

This venue has operated as a restaurant for many years despite an awkward location—atop a hill on a busy corner in a suburban residential neighborhood—and for years different owners cycled in and out, never able to make it work. It even operated under the name the White Elephant for a period. Eventually in the '80s, a

French family purchased the property and turned it into one of the premiere French provincial restaurants in the region.

It is still a very classy French restaurant thirty-plus years later. And they cater to a demographic who greatly appreciates the service and atmosphere. My impression is they have adapted to ensure a continued clientele. With the advent of Groupon, they are bringing in a new group of potential customers. Very smart, and a great way to survive. We can't wait to return ourselves!

My local taxi company does airport runs, and I use them quite frequently. Their fleet is *old* and often smells of stale cigarettes. But they are a neighborhood business run and staffed by local employees, and their timing is impeccable (which is extremely important for airport transportation). On a recent trip, as I got into the car, I thought, "Jeez, I should really think about finding a more upscale airport transport service." But a few minutes into the ride, the driver and I struck up a conversation, as often happens with the gents from this company. We talked about a variety of topics: US politics, life on Mars, his dream of someday moving to New Zealand, the meaning of life—let's just say I got quite an education on that ride. Suddenly I was transported from that slightly stinky car to places I had never thought much about. It certainly distracted me from my jet-lagged fatigue and exhaustion.

So on second thought, I decided to stay with my mom-and-pop taxi service. They have served me well over the years, always offering lively conversation and reasonable fares. And, after all, they are local, reliable, and, I must say, pretty darn entertaining for the weary but attentive traveler.

To achieve success, managers must build the teams and infrastructure to support the delivery of highly valued, outstanding products and services. Creating something special and differentiated is the key to building a brand!

CHAPTER FIVE:
Inspire Through Mentorship

Mentorship is an individual relationship in which two people learn from each other. In its best form, it's symbiotic. In fact, we should call both people in a mentoring relationship *mentors* because they *always* mutually benefit. In my years of mentoring, most if not all the dilemmas brought to me by my mentees have been the exact struggles I was facing myself, in different contexts. By working through them with my mentees, I've been able to visualize and then verbalize the solutions. Pretty cool, I must say. It's almost cosmic when it happens.

Mentoring starts with a willingness to help.

In 2019, I was in Walt Disney World for a softball spring training trip with our high school varsity softball team. I missed the first game to conduct a global video conference—the closest I will ever get to being one of those Disney starlets livestreaming from "The World."

I was feeling a tiny bit sorry for myself until I ran into one of the coaches at the food court the next day at 6:45 a.m. It hit me like a ton of bricks: these coaches (from a multitude of schools) sacrificed their entire spring break to give the teams a chance to play competitively on incredible ESPN fields, then spend the second eight hours of their day at the parks.

The level of dedication I witnessed over those few days as a chaperone was inspirational. People who spend their lives helping others "improve their game" are my heroes. Whether you're on the field, in the classroom, putting together a presentation, or just being a mentor, taking your knowledge and sharing it with others is a gift of limitless proportions. For a moment, I wished I had chosen a different path. Then I realized you don't have to choose a career as a coach or teacher to have that type of impact. It's available to all who have the drive to help other people do better. Pay it forward, and you might be someone's hero!

What Does Mentorship Look Like?

» It's Not a One-Way Street

People come to me for advice all the time. It is an honor, frankly, and I take these requests very seriously. But quite often the advice I am giving out is relevant to my own situation, and in a roundabout way, my colleagues are bringing to me the exact puzzles I need to solve for myself. Ironically, I often don't heed my own advice. It's a classic case of knowing what to do but not doing it. Someone came to me recently, and my advice was, "Put together a five-year plan.

Because five years is really a timeline you can plan, and beyond that there are too many variables." But do you think I have a five-year plan? *No!* I most certainly do not (not documented, anyway).

On a positive note, however, I think I have convinced myself at this point—and thankfully I can be quite persuasive. If you didn't catch it yet, I am telling you too: make sure you have a plan. One year, five years—whatever works to help you start achieving your goals.

Mentoring is good for the soul. I had a recent session with my main mentor to talk about short- and long-term goals. Mixed into the conversation were all kinds of anecdotes, morsels of wisdom, and references to past experiences. At one point, he said to me, "Caroline, you write all sorts of inspiring things—you don't need me." Of course, I do need mentoring just as much as anyone. And my dirty little secret is that much of what I write is to give myself a reminder too—of what is important and what I should focus on in my daily travels.

It was incredibly helpful to me, and as I thanked him, he thanked me back and said, "I think this helped me as much as it helped you!" I understand that sentiment! Every time I mentor someone, they ask questions that cause me to reach into my personal library of experiences. It digs up ideas I haven't thought of in a while and gives me great reminders of how to approach my career and profession. So while it is always great to have your own mentor(s), don't be afraid to mentor others. You just might learn something too!

My mentees continue to bring me their versions of the very issues I have been dealing with myself. And there is no better way to work through a tough moment than by trying to see something similar through someone else's eyes. When I hear my words telling them what they should do, I am actually telling myself too. Eerie stuff. But helpful—and productive.

Being a mentor is not a one-way street. It can be a hugely rewarding and motivating experience. I highly recommend it, especially if you sometimes struggle yourself and have a deeper understanding of the emotional side of work. And, of course, solving your own problems is a bonus!

» Listening Goes a Long Way

Shortly after my dad, Paul, passed away, I received an urgent message from a former neighbor I hadn't heard from in thirty years. She wanted to share a story about Paul's influence on her life. I was quite anxious to hear how a cherished friend remembered him.

She first moved to New York in 1974 as a young pioneer in the technology field. As neighbors, she and Paul would frequently commute to or from NYC together. At the time, she was quite a fish out of water—an Indian woman in a very male-dominated business and a rare mom working outside the home, without much of a community support structure. But over the course of many train rides to NYC, she confided in Paul about the challenges she faced. He listened intently, offered words of encouragement, and helped fuel the confidence she needed to be successful. She wanted to share with me how much she appreciated his forward-thinking and accepting outlook all those years ago.

My dad was born on May 8, 1921—Mother's Day! That meant that every few years, his birthday celebration would be preempted for his mom. Until he had kids, and then it was preempted for his wife. Then they had a daughter who was born in May, and, well, you know the rest.

He was a proud Taurus—the bull—rarely standing for any "bull." Luckily for me, his father had been a successful business-man whose travails had taken him on the road, leaving my dad behind in a household very much run by his strong-willed mother, whose name, interestingly enough, was Grace. During those years, he had learned to honor the authority of the woman he called Mom and ultimately developed a deep respect for women in the workplace as a result.

Our neighbor revealed that my dad had been a daily cheer-leader and advocate as she'd built an incredible career in the nascent computer industry.

In a way, my father was an accidental mentor—never intend-ing, to my knowledge, to have any particular influence over any-one's career. In fact, as I recall, he struggled greatly in building his own. But his legacy shows the power of his actions: a grateful friend who built confidence with the support of his faith and inspi-ration. A happy accident indeed!

» It Sometimes Takes a Push

Advice is great, but many of us (not me, of course!) tend toward pigheadedness and resist, thinking we don't need help. It reminds me of a scene from *Planes, Trains and Automobiles* when Steve Martin and John Candy get turned around on a dark highway, and drivers on the other side of the median are screaming over and over again: "You're going the wrong way!"

Martin and Candy look at each other and say, "How do they know where we are going?" and brush it off, only to realize they are absolutely on the wrong side of the highway.

I had an experience like this once after some years out of the workforce. A former colleague called. She had a role that might work for me because I could spend a few days per week at home. Interesting. But I went to the interview and was, I don't know, nonplussed? Scared? I left the meeting and called my husband.

"How did it go?" he asked.

"I don't know; I'm not sure I'm that into it."

A pause, and then he said, "Well, you *get* into it. They are giving you an opportunity after being out of the market for a while. You *get* into it!"

I hung up and immediately emailed my contact. "I'm interested!" Thankfully, that time I listened and acted. Sometimes others really do need to tell us what to do. And we must listen!

Making a Difference by Jumping in to Help

Recently, I was thinking about a headhunter who contacted me in the mid-2000s whose name I cannot remember for the life of me. At the time I was a relatively new mom with two small kids, dreaming of reentering the workforce after a few years away, and this man had taken an interest in my story. Right off the bat, he sent me on a couple of interviews, but the gap in my résumé (about three years at that point) was a problem. The roles I was interviewing for were more junior than what I had left, but the employers were still skeptical.

One day after a successful visit to the mall to tire out the kids before nap time, I was driving home, and this headhunter called my cell phone. (This was well before smartphones or even electronic contact lists, so I seriously don't have a record of him anywhere.) I pulled over with two dozing babies in the back seat. He wanted to talk about some ideas for getting me back to work. He spent a good half hour reviewing some opportunities with me and also asking me questions about my background and what I wanted to do. He seemed energized by the challenge my particular situation presented. I was overjoyed that someone professional was taking me seriously, as it had not taken long after leaving the workforce for my confidence to wane and my hopes to fade.

Mentoring, encouragement, support—all really good things that can make a huge impact on someone's life. Fifteen minutes, a half hour of your time—it can make all the difference to a colleague or friend in need. The help I received from this headhunter all those years ago was a spark that turned into some courage that eventually led me back to full-time work and a career I love. If only I could remember his name and reach out to thank him!

Fast-forward to a few years ago, when I was about to interview for a new role that would be a great move for me—the kind of shift that would launch my career in a completely different direction. In passing, I told a senior leader at the firm about my upcoming meeting, and he offered to help. I wasn't astonished—he was someone who was always eager to pitch in—but I was nonetheless flattered by his generosity. He had just started a new role and was extremely busy. But that was no issue, he made clear to me.

We happened to both live near the beach in the same town, so we decided to walk and talk. He brought a mug of coffee from his home. I remember nervously checking to make sure his coffee didn't slosh over the rim onto his hand. We stopped at a bench for a few minutes to take in the scenery while we chatted. He said it was important to do so.

He knew the players I would be meeting and was able to shed light on what he thought they would be looking for. I shared with him some feedback—that the initial concern was that I was a bit reserved. I must have said it in a slightly defensive way, and he said, "Well, you are! Let's turn it into a strength." He asked me the questions he thought they would ask. He made me think and rethink through my answers. All in all, we spent an hour together. I was amazed at the kindness of that.

Incredibly, I went to the interview, and all we talked about was family, the state of politics, Walt Disney World, and a little bit of sports. It turned out the confidence I projected through preparation was all they were looking for (on top of my experience, of course). I got the job and a newfound career path. Gratitude to the mentorship of my colleague for helping me build the confidence I needed to succeed!

CHAPTER SIX:
Find the Courage to Lead

Managers make sure the trains run on time and are fully staffed to deliver the service. But leaders set the tone for how that service will be delivered. Ideally, they create an environment in which employees do their best work, and they lay the groundwork for expanding the business, building opportunities for new teams along the way.

A friend asked me, "What do you think is the most important quality in a leader?"

Two ideas came to me: courage and compassion. But ultimately, I chose courage. One thing I have found is that when leaders don't have compassion, they usually lack courage too. Courage can be the key to unlocking many other important leadership qualities:

- **C**ompassion
- **O**bjectivity
- **U**nderstanding
- **R**esilience
- **A**daptability
- **G**race
- **E**mpathy

These are my principles of leadership. It seems all those qualities are contained within courage after all!

Lack of courage makes leaders do bad things to their employees and drive them away. How do you build courage? Put yourself in uncomfortable situations. Uncover the truth in a lifelong mystery. Make a call you really don't want to make. A whole lot of small victories add up to muscle—the strength you will need to pursue the bigger challenges. Building blocks don't have to be bricks with perfect ninety-degree edges. They can be pebbles, stones, jagged-edged rocks . . . the point is when you add them up, you have a structure of strength that can support you—and allow you to lead with courage!

How Do You Recognize Great Leaders?

» They Roll Up Their Sleeves and Pitch In

During my childhood, my parents were good friends with the CEO of one of the top advertising agencies in the world. He was a heavy hitter in his business but a real down-to-earth guy at home. One night he and his family came to our house for dinner. At the end of the meal, this executive donned an apron and went to work cleaning the dishes. He even quipped that he really shouldn't do us this favor because the dishwashing liquid we stocked was not his client's brand. Nonetheless, he finished the chore, and the evening ended with everyone in great spirits.

This story has stuck with me through the years—I was impressed that someone of his stature would so readily pitch in. To me it speaks volumes about his character and ability to recognize where help is needed. So tell me, leaders: Are you willing to roll up your sleeves?

I'll never forget the time . . . I was new to the JLL corporate office, having only ever worked on-site with clients. As I stood staring at the copy machine one day, one of the most senior brokers in the office came over and said, "Do you need help?" He proceeded to show me how to use the machine, then took me to his office to show me the different printing options. All in all, it took less than ten minutes but saved me a lot of time trying to figure things out myself.

You're never too important or successful to help a colleague!

» They Care for Their Teams

The first time I heard the term *people care* was during a sales meeting. We wanted to convey the importance of people care when absorbing incumbent employees for new contracts. It made sense—our clients recognize that the people are truly everything in our business.

Every year on Mother's Day, I find myself thinking back to twenty-plus years ago when I was not yet a mother, and my boss used to call me Mom. He was twenty-plus years older than me, and this was his term of endearment for me. Perhaps because I always took care of my team? I don't know. Back then there was not much chatter about people care in the business world. So when a truly caring manager showed up, it was something special. Maybe that is still true today, now that I think of it.

The Mom theme has continued. As mentioned, I once had an employee seven years younger than me who told me, "You're like a mother to me." Uh-huh. There was another role more recently in which my right-hand man and I were frequently referred to as Mom and Dad. What gives with this? Books have been written about how you shouldn't mother people at work. I wonder if they asked the people who were on the receiving end of that nurturing their opinion. Either way, we often see our colleagues as our "work family": work wives, work husbands, etc. Is it so bad if we have work moms and dads too? Families are associated with care, after all.

People care became the entire focus of my role during the pandemic—ensuring my team had the support, tools, and resources they needed every day. I once had a manager who argued with me that delivering the financials was the number one responsibility of my job. I said no—building and supporting the team was the most important because without it, we would never have a chance of delivering the financials. He was incredulous, and we never agreed on that point. But I stand by those statements, especially in light of recent events. I remember one time having lunch with him and a couple of colleagues and saying that if I could survive my current role, I could literally do "anything." It was a tough position and account for a long list of reasons, and I was really feeling the pain.

My manager looked at me and said, "It's not about survival. It's about delivering." Wow!

Thinking back on this, I see that my comment was not exactly a cry for help but perhaps more of a window into how I was feeling. When an employee reveals they are in survival mode, they need support. They need someone to have their back. As leaders, we need to be aware of these things and address them, not double down on the corporate speak.

I left that manager and never looked back. Except to think of it and realize what I needed to do for my team. Now, having gone through the COVID-19 crisis, I can't imagine I would have ever told any team member that financials or client service was more important than what they were feeling. Take care of your people, and they will take care of business! Providing structure, support, encouragement, and guidance is everything, especially when facing difficult circumstances. By the way, as you may have guessed, I did survive. And I do believe I can do anything! (So can you.)

We know our business is strong when we have great teams who love their jobs and are dedicated to their clients. People care gets them there!

» They Are Standing By to Support

Giving your team autonomy helps them build the skills and confidence they need to succeed. Knowing that you are nearby and able to help in a pinch gives them a lifeline of support "just in case." Micromanagement is not the key—sometimes you simply have to stand by and let others lead or make decisions, even if it is not exactly the way you would do it.

On a recent trip to the grocery store, my items totaled up to $12.91. I gave the cashier $13, then said, "Oh wait, let me give you a penny so you can give me a dime."

He took the cash and opened the register. A look of frustration came over his face, and he said, "I am sorry, but I only have nickels" as he handed two to me.

It reminded me that we as leaders must not be too quick to prescribe the process when a new project comes online. Instead, we should focus on the outcomes and let our employees define the way forward. For a split second I unnecessarily made this young cashier feel like he was not meeting my expectations. Two nickels or a dime—either way I was getting my ten cents. He didn't need me to tell him how to do it. And neither do my employees!

Leaders often get stuck with ugly assignments. One Friday, my husband and I took our two daughters to a lovely dinner at a local restaurant owned by a big-time celebrity. A good time was had by all. That was the fun part. When we came home, my eldest daughter announced that her gecko was getting too skinny and she had therefore bought him some "super worms." Super worms, unlike mealworms, do not survive refrigeration. Mealworms are refrigerated to slow down the metamorphosis process and their movement in general.

Daughter number one produced a carton with holes in the top that was labeled "Super Worms." I didn't know what to expect, but I noticed she was acting very anxious and nervous about removing the top (which would be required to serve up the worms to the gecko). We could hear them moving around in there. Daughter number two entered and agreed to remove the top. I was on standby, not volunteering for any of it. Daughter number two nervously removed the top, and a gaggle of *large disgusting worms* was seen squirming to get out of the carton. They were spilling over the top! I looked up and noticed that I was suddenly the only person in the room. I quickly replaced the top after a few worms escaped. I removed the worm carton from the scene. All that was heard was screaming from the other room while I was completing these activities.

The moral? As leaders, we sometimes need to stand by and let our teams do the work. They may not always individually have all the right skills to complete a task, but together they can be unstoppable. And then there will be those times when you are left holding the proverbial bag (or carton, as it were). The key is to be there for them when they need us, available to jump in at a moment's notice. Even if it's ugly business (which it most certainly was in this case)!

Leaders who always define the way forward are missing out. There is good stuff brewing in the brains of their team members. If you have a diverse team from varying backgrounds, even better. They will bring multiple different perspectives to a problem and find great solutions if you just let them be. If they reach the breaking point and need to call in your expertise—well, that's what you are there for. But let them try first on their own; they will undoubtedly grow skills and creativity and may even avoid catastrophic results such as super worms making a grand escape . . .

How Can You Lead Your Team to Success?

» Support and Encourage Your Team

When I think of my role as a leader, one thing that comes to mind is an experience I had in college when I played on the rugby team for about two-tenths of a second.

Originally, I joined the team for two reasons: there were some very cool, strong women on the team, and there was beer drinking involved. I was assigned to be a prop, which thankfully was not a big running position. Ultimately, my job during a scrum was to get in position quickly on one side of the kicker (hooker) to ensure she had enough support to kick the ball with force and advance our team. This is truly what I do for my team every day: making sure I can quickly move into position when needed to support their individual success as well as the success of the team.

Well, I didn't last as a rugby player—I am not much of an athlete—but when it comes to leading teams, this "prop" support role is where it's at for me. And ironically in my current role, running (from meeting to meeting) is a sport in and of itself!

On a recent workday, someone told me I had lifted their spirits. In a stressful and busy week where there were definitely some highs and lows, this made me feel great. Then I went running one morning, and I saw a ton of lawn signs in my hometown that had red hearts on them. It got me thinking about how love is an essential part of leadership. In fact, I would go so far as to say that if you can't lead with love and empathy in your heart, you have no business being a leader.

Later in the week, I had a brief back-and-forth with a colleague about being nice and how sometimes it bites you in the, ahem, "rear end."

He said, "Yes, I have lots of bite marks." I am sure this person does. But, I concluded, so what? I'll take the bites if it means I make one person's life a little easier. There is enough stress in the world—more than plenty to go around. I'm going to focus on lifting spirits and improving lives. And I'll invest in a pillow to soothe my sore caboose!

In 2020, I had the pleasure of participating in an executive panel before a group of JLL "Big Bet" talent—folks the firm is investing in as future leaders. The format is informal: a panel of four, a moderator, and a series of questions meant to evoke thoughtful answers that often turn out to be inspirational as well. I always learn something from my colleagues during these discussions, and this time was no different.

The first question was, What does leadership mean to you? My answer was that leaders need to lead with empathy and love in their hearts. I have listened to many leaders say "Business first!" or "Clients first!" But to me, it's "People first!" Get that right, and everything else will fall into place. Easy (ish).

» Just Be Normal

A few weeks ago, during a team meeting, I presented an escalator "safety moment." Safety moments are a tool we use in facilities and property management to encourage a culture of health and safety. We choose a topic and highlight its importance in risk management. To add some levity to an otherwise ho-hum topic, I told a story about one of my own escalator experiences, which happened in a McDonald's in Times Square. I was eighteen and boarded the moving stairway with my tray piled high with a Big Mac, french fries, and a rather tall soda. The punch line of the story is that I made it all the way to the top (quite a feat), then fell butt-over-tea-kettle forward and dropped my entire tray, spilling Diet Coke all the way down to the ground floor. One of the klutzier showings of my life.

A day or two later I read on LinkedIn that studies show that when male leaders tell self-deprecating stories, they are seen as *relatable*, and when female leaders do so, they are seen as *weak* and *incompetent*. Well, this was very bad news for me, since that is about 90 percent of my schtick—always poking fun at myself (tons of material).

I immediately thought, "Seriously? Are they really thinking I am weak and incompetent because of *this*? It can't be." And I expect much more from my colleagues. But more importantly, as a leader, you need to be authentic. Don't get caught posing as something you aren't. Someone out there will find you *relatable* (male *or* female you may be). I promise!

I was at a company leadership summit in February of 2020, participating as a panelist to discuss the concept that we are "Better Together." It was all about cross-pollinating our services, expanding our internal networks, and building business together as one team. Important to reinforce in a company with multiple service lines that should be but aren't always easily integrated.

Backstage while I was getting miked up, I found myself nose to nose with one of the senior-most people in our organization. He immediately started a casual conversation and made me feel at ease with a little humor. I came away thinking, "Wow, we are lucky to have this person leading our company."

Firms around the world are spending literally billions every year to promote greater collaboration. But what if we also just treat each other nicely and put each other at ease? What if we break down the barriers between us and our businesses with kindness? I have news for you—it's free! It doesn't cost a red cent. Maybe I am oversimplifying. Or maybe I'm not. This executive I chatted with the other day seems to be doing just fine using that tactic. It appears to have served him quite well!

» Encourage Inspiration

When I was in college, I worked at a summer camp and was responsible for forty-two girls, ages twelve through thirteen, and the ten associated staff. It was our first staff meeting. (Two days earlier, three of my team had *almost* been arrested for shoplifting at Caldor but for the kindness of the security guards, so I had my work cut out for me with this nice but slightly misguided crew.) Our focus was to schedule the daily classes; each staff member would teach two electives. You could literally make them up—some examples I offered were "Juggling" and "Teach Caroline to Dance." It had to be fun and fill forty-five minutes.

Silence, grunts, and complaints. "I don't know how to do anything," they said.

I asked, "Can you play soccer? Teach it! Can you tell stories? Teach it!" I finally said, "C'mon, ladies—get up your gumption!" That made them laugh, and we eventually squeezed out enough ideas to fill the schedule.

Sometimes people need a push to be creative. A leader's job is to pry open the door to that creativity. Fear, lack of confidence, inability to focus—any number of these barriers can stand in the way of your team. Set the example, and take the first step. By the way, I still don't know how to dance, but the kids sure had fun trying to teach me!

In 2020, when I spoke on an executive panel to discuss leadership with some of the most promising up-and-coming leaders at JLL, one of the questions had to do with status quo: How do you encourage creative thinking to help drive change? My answer was that I speak up. I ask questions. And then I offer solutions. I'm never satisfied with "the way we always do things." It's a fact:

people always say they want change, but the truth is they don't. They resist. So it is important to highlight what needs to change and find ways to mitigate risks.

Another question for the panel was about who inspired us. Well, that's easy. My two daughters are my greatest inspiration— and every time I am faced with a status quo challenge, I think of them and the fact that I need to speak up to make things better for their future. If I don't, who will? I can't rely on others.

Great leaders understand what makes their teams tick. Their motivations, their cares and dislikes, and what inspires them. Leaders can pull this information out of their teams by sharing their personal pillars of inspiration. This is where leaders need to be vulnerable. The ability to be vulnerable shows grace and courage. It also shows strength. Weak leaders can't reveal the truth about themselves and don't deserve to know the truth about their teams either. It starts at the top—modeling the confidence to share what matters most in our career journeys. *That* can be simultaneously inspiring and motivating for teams.

"If you see something, say something." As a leader, I certainly hope you will say something to me someday about what you think needs to change. Let's have a discussion and solve it together!

On the topic of inspiration, I had an important presentation one day, so the night before, I found myself scouring the internet for something inspirational to send my team to get them excited. I was unsuccessful! So I turned my attention to finding my own inspiration.

What I realized quickly was that looking up "inspirational movie speeches" brings you to pretty much the same hits as if you looked up "inspirational sports speeches." Disappointing because not all of us connect well with sports. So I turned to my own personal go-to for inspiration. That's right; I started digging into Broadway and movie musicals. It turns out inspiration is very personal, and it's hard to find a one-size-fits-all alternative. So here is what I have to say: Find what inspires you, and make sure it is a part of your regular "intake" of soul nourishment. As a leader, I will still try to find "general" inspiration for my team, but they each know best what gets their heart beating.

Maybe you wonder what I listened to. I sought out "Climb Every Mountain" from *The Sound of Music*, multiple songs from *Rent*, and "Everybody Rejoice/Brand New Day" from *The Wiz*. And, of course, "Defying Gravity" from *Wicked*. All so great. So tell me: What do you do for inspiration?

» Allow Your Team to Lead

One of my colleagues made a statement that I really liked. Everyone is a leader. We don't need to defer to a single figurehead, but rather, we can gain knowledge, wisdom, and guidance from multiple sources at every level. *Yes!* And imagine how it makes someone feel and fosters their growth when you seek their help. Leaders aren't born—they are grown. We can help our colleagues become leaders by encouraging them to lead us. Oh, it's so simple—why didn't I think of it? It's okay; someone else did, and I learned. And grew a little too!

» Use Your Influence

Some people reading may be skeptical because they have seen people ascend to leadership positions who do not deserve to be there. The sad truth is that is not limited to the business world. It is a reality we must all live with. And most of those people will do everything within their power to maintain their positions, stepping on anyone who tries to expose them. This is something I have experienced firsthand, and it is frustrating, but I don't let it deter me. You shouldn't either! Instead, I put my focus on using the influence I have to chip away at the status quo.

At my last team meeting, I showcased a quote by Shirley Chisholm for Black History Month: "If they don't give you a seat at the table, bring a folding chair." Love it—you don't need to wait to be invited! Then someone sent me this quote: "Never beg for a seat when you can build your own table." Who needs people who want to exclude? You can build your own success! And in a final follow-up, a team member sent me this: "I say 'Never beg for anything' . . . just do it better so 'they' will be chasing you to join them!" All good stuff to think about as leaders trying to make a difference. Go out there, and get a piece of the action!

» **Think Positive**

The first lesson from my statistics professor in business school was that you can make the numbers say whatever you want. So when I glimpsed a stat on the Captivate screen in my building's elevator one morning showing that "1 in 3 girls is scared to lead because they don't want to be seen as bossy," I had to laugh. Are you kidding me? *Bossy* has a negative connotation—I wonder what the boys responded. I am betting their numbers were similar. We'll never know. But what I really liked about this stat was when I flipped it around and realized that two in three girls don't give a "blank" if you see them as bossy because they want to lead. *Yeah!* That's what that statistic says to me, and I'm good with it.

Leadership takes courage. Strong leadership is not about a thirst for power—those leaders are weak and scared. For a long time in my career, I was happy being the number two on the team. I wasn't ready for the level of responsibility that came with being number one. But what I realized later is that I was still leading in those roles and serving as a mentor to the people on my team. Everyone can be a leader, even in support roles, and if we band together, we can influence the way our lives are shaped in the future—at work, at home, or in our leisure activities. The people around us will want to follow our lead and learn through mentorship how to emulate our grace.

CHAPTER SEVEN:
Moving Forward

One night when it was far too late into the evening and I was a little bored, I happened upon a YouTube video of my high school graduation—wow! As you may realize, my high school graduation took place "some moons ago," well before smart-phones, when videotaping an occasion was a very big deal. I had no recollection of there being a videographer (that's the person with the camera, FYI) at graduation. Turns out there were multiple, as evidenced by the varied angles. But I digress.

Of course, I watched the entire thing (not the speeches). A parade of classmates from way back when, knowing only perhaps where they would attend school or work the following fall—but beyond that were just heaps of dreams and aspirations. The angelic faces (even on the devilish ones!) were full of promise and hope. I shed a tear for the four classmates we have already lost but felt glee thinking of all the accomplishments over the years since that day as the names were read and the smiles were flashed.

It's not easy to build a career, but when you do it in small steps at your own pace and put in the necessary time, you can achieve amazing results.

Math was a subject that I loved but always found challenging. I had a math teacher in high school who had a unique way of approaching difficult problems. His name was Mr. Sadlon. He looked like Meathead from *All in the Family* and smelled like stale cigarettes. He always wore a tie but no jacket and a rather large signet ring on his right hand.

Mr. Sadlon would approach the toughest trig or advanced algebra problems in a very deadpan way. The guy was never agitated, though his students were regularly squirming in their seats. He would take us through a problem, and at the end, once he'd received everyone's approval and understanding, he would write on the board "QED." He said it stood for "Quite Easily Done," but it really stood for the Latin *quod erat demonstrandum* ("which was shown or demonstrated"). But he meant it was Quite Easily Done. Math didn't have to be hard if you put in the time. In fact, it could be easy.

As you embark on the next phase of your journey, I encourage you to hearken back to those joyful days of youth and summon that feeling of excited anticipation for the future I saw in my high school graduation video. Every day can be the first day of the rest of your life. If you need to make changes, it's okay to start small. Bank some wins, and move on to increasingly bigger challenges. Set goals, and surround yourself with people who can help you achieve them.

There will be challenges for you along the way—some will seem too hard or too scary. But when you successfully tackle them, think of Mr. Sadlon: QED. It will never be as tough as you think as long as you put in the time!

Made in United States
Orlando, FL
07 June 2022

18573441R00080